Confessions
OF A TEACHER RECRUITER

How to Create an Extraordinary Resume and Hook Your Dream Job

the
opportunities
project

By Tracy L. Brisson
Founder, The Opportunities Project

TABLE OF CONTENTS

Legal Stuff 4

Hello, Teachers! 5

Introduction: Some Tough Love 7

Chapter One: Busting Myths About the Hiring Process 9

Chapter Two: Differentiating Yourself from Your Peers 20

Chapter Three: Creating Your Extraordinary Resume Section by Section 27

Chapter Four: Making Your Resume Pretty 46

Chapter Five: The True Purpose of Cover Letters 52

Chapter Six: The Benefits of Social Media and Digital Portfolios 56

Chapter Seven: Tips for Overcoming Job Search Anxiety 70

Chapter Eight: Final Don'ts and Do's and Sample Documents 75

Acknowledgements 84

About The Opportunities Project and Tracy Brisson 86

Contact Information 87

Tracy's Tip!

Throughout this book I'll offer you tips and suggestions to get the most out of the content. Here is my first one on how to best engage with the material.

You may be short on time and be tempted to jump straight to Chapter Three and its shiny title of "Creating Your Extraordinary Resume Section by Section. I suggest you do not skip ahead and instead read the book in the order it's presented. The information in the first two chapters will provide you with a competitive advantage most applicants don't have. **You won't create an extraordinary resume if you skip these fundamental lessons and exercises.**

Reading the lessons and doing the exercises should take between five and ten hours. You can do this work in one-to-two hour sessions over one-to-two weeks. **I suggest that you find your calendar and schedule this time now.**

LEGAL STUFF

COPYRIGHT:

Confessions of a Teacher Recruiter: How to Create an Extraordinary Resume and Hook Your Dream Job is governed by the Creative Commons License Attribution-NonCommercial-ShareAlike 3.0 United States (CC BY-NC-SA 3.0). You are not permitted to use this work for your own commercial purposes. If you share any part of this work, it must be attributed to The Opportunities Project.

EBOOK LICENSE AGREEMENT:

The Opportunities Project and/or SEAM Publishing has authorized you to download one copy of this electronic book (ebook). The Opportunities Project grants you a nonexclusive, nontransferable license to use the ebook for your individual purpose.

This License Agreement permits you to download the ebook for your use only.

You shall not: (1) resell, rent, assign, timeshare, distribute, or transfer all or part of the ebook or any rights granted hereunder to any other person; (2) duplicate the ebook, except for a single backup or archival copy; (3) remove any proprietary notices, labels, or marks from the ebook; or (4) transfer or sublicense the title to the ebook to any other party.

The ebook is owned by The Opportunities Project and is protected by United States and international copyright and other intellectual property laws. This license and your right to use the ebook terminate automatically if you violate any part of this Agreement.

If you are interested in purchasing bulk licenses of this ebook or print versions, please contact The Opportunities Project at info@oppsproject.com for purchasing information.

HELLO TEACHERS!

Spring 2013

Dear Teacher,

Thanks for purchasing my book *Confessions of a Teacher Recruiter: How to Create an Extraordinary Resume and Hook Your Dream Job.* I am excited to share my knowledge with teachers committed to helping young people succeed and wrote this book to give you the know-how you need to sell yourself in the job search process.

While my advice here is targeted toward teachers, it can be useful to anyone who wants to create a resume that stands out in a crowded field. In 2011, there were 3.7 million teachers actively working in the United States. **Hundreds of people applied for the 8% of positions that were filled that year.** The National Association of Colleges and Employers (NACE) reported that in 2010 only 24% of new graduates who majored in education received a full-time offer before September. This was 11% lower than the placement rate for journalism majors, a field many have romanticized as the hardest of all to enter.

In every school district I have worked in or consulted with, less than 15% of applicants were hired in any given year. **Finding a teaching job in 2013 is cutthroat competitive.**

I think it's a good idea to start our journey together by telling you about my teacher recruitment and career coaching experience, and why I feel I am qualified to help you create a resume that tells people how awesome you are and demands the attention of those who have the power to hire you.

I started recruiting teachers almost 13 years ago after two years of teaching fourth and sixth grade as a Teach For America corps member in the Washington Heights section of New York City. There were plenty of things I loved about teaching, including Anthony, Glendy, and Josue, among others, and I am grateful to catch glimpses of their adult lives on Facebook. My students and I worked well together, which was evident when I received a Project Smart Exemplary Teaching Award from the New York City Department of Education.

But my first confession to you is that I found that being a classroom teacher was not a fit for me. I was good at some aspects of teaching, yet not so great at others. I am a person who loves adventure and starting new things, and students need routine.

Despite my undecided future plans, I left the classroom with the understanding that there is no greater investment we can make in our country's economic future than hiring excellent teachers.

A year after leaving the classroom (and starting a plan to become a tax attorney with big dreams of revising the nation's tax code) I was unexpectedly invited to join the founding program team for the NYC Teaching Fellows, an alternative teacher certification program aimed at career changers. The program recruited close to 3,000 teachers annually in its first few years and today, 11% of all the New York City's public school teachers started their career as a NYC Teaching Fellow.

In 2002, a few months after 9/11, the Fellows program received over 20,000 applications from individuals all over the country and in every industry who wanted to come to New York City and make a difference. The conversations with people who were willing to uproot their entire lives for our kids after that painful event impacted me deeply and changed my career path permanently. I became an eternal fan of teachers and dedicated myself back to education.

Over the last 13 years, **I've reviewed more than 20,000 teacher resumes** starting in my early days with the NYC Teaching Fellows, then as the Director of Teacher Recruitment for all of New York City's 1,600+ public schools, and next as a private recruitment consultant for charters, school districts, and foundations that support teachers such as the Newark Public Schools and the Woodrow Wilson National Fellowship Foundation. On top of all this, I have helped hundreds of teachers rewrite their resumes through individual and group career coaching since I founded The Opportunities Project in 2010.

When it comes to teacher resumes, I know the extraordinary, the ugly, and, worst of all, the mediocre. I am determined to make your resume fall unequivocally into the extraordinary category.

Once you've digested the advice, tips, and exercises in this book, I know you'll become one of the teachers who principals fight over during the hiring season. Let's get started.

Best,

Tracy

Tracy Brisson
Founder, The Opportunities Project

INTRODUCTION: SOME TOUGH LOVE

My letter to teachers hopefully left you with a sense of hope! We're going to do it! But before we start, I would like to share some tough love with you.

I want every reader of this book to get the job he or she desires and rock in it, but we have to start where you are. It is highly possible that some of your resumes... well, stink.

A good reason your resume may stink is that you've received little career guidance. If you are a career changer or experienced teacher, it may have been many years since you've had to apply for a job. If you are a recent college graduate, the quality of services you received from your career center may have been lacking.

Here's my second confession as a teacher recruiter: recruiters love to share stories about terrible resumes, and I am no different. Once I received a resume from an English teacher who crashed my inbox by inserting into his resume a 10MB photo of himself looking drunk at a party. Another time, I sat at my desk confused by the resume from the 33-year-old candidate who listed her middle school Presidential Fitness award on page eight. I only know her age because her birth date was on page five.

Almost every organization I've worked with who hires teachers has a wall of shame where they post resumes that feature clip art. Seriously, no more apples on your resume. Stop.

However entertaining these terrible resumes may be, they are the minority. The overwhelming majority of resumes and cover letters are mediocre and often passed over. Many candidates may have been really interesting people who could change students' lives, but the resumes were cluttered, disorganized, and didn't tell a story specific and unique to them. And that makes me sad because it's a waste all around.

Mediocre resumes are the worst. At least resumes that stink are memorable.

Recruiters have constraints. Our time is literally measured in money. A recent client received over 600 resumes for only 20 elementary teacher positions. My client, the person who pays my bills, hired me to find the absolute best teachers in the most efficient way possible. My goal is not to fairly evaluate every applicant in depth. If I did that, I'd never finish on time or on budget.

While we may smile at you at recruitment events and make you feel invigorated and welcome, it's important to remember that our teacher recruitment work is not altruism. **We are in the business of picking the best teachers from the pool.**

I considered titling this book "Make Me Want to Hire You to Teach My Children," because that is the high standard I apply in hiring. Would I put you in a classroom in front of my nephew and niece, James and Lily, the most treasured kids in my life?

If you cannot convince me you would be amazing for the children in my family, you cannot work with my clients' students either.

So why all this negativity to start? It's essential that you understand what you're up against before you make the first edit on your resume. Having the right mindset, and committing to demonstrating excellence at every stage of the recruitment process, is what will lead to your dream job.

Now that we are on the same page, let's transition back into the good, inspirational stuff: making your resume extraordinary and getting the job you want.

CHAPTER ONE: BUSTING MYTHS ABOUT THE HIRING PROCESS

Bad career advice drives me bonkers. **Some of the worst resume advice is perpetuated by human resources and career services professionals.** There. I said it.

If you listen to some "experts," you'll believe incorrect assumptions about how your resume is used in the recruitment and selection process. Here are a few of those incorrect assumptions.

- Resumes are only good for being pulled apart by the application system where you submit applications (called an Applicant Tracking System [ATS] by us recruiter people).

- The sole purpose of the ATS is to search resumes for highly customized keywords, so pack as many as you can in if you want to get noticed—even hide them in the margins in white font if you must!

- These super smart ATS's hate formatting, so don't you dare try to make your resume look nice.

- Applying through the ATS and waiting for us to get back to you is the only way you can get a job in our school district. **Don't bother us again until we contact you.**

If you have heard these myths about job searching and accepted them as fact, you might be on a curvy path that is leaving you frustrated and possibly unemployed. This chapter debunks these and other hiring myths and reviews the details about the teacher hiring process that will help you gain a competitive advantage over other applicants.

Let's make it our goal to remove all roadblocks in your way, starting with incorrect thinking. What follows is a series of questions I often hear from teachers and corresponding answers that will set you straight.

What is this Applicant Tracking System thing?

An Applicant Tracking System (ATS) is the system that recruiters use to manage the selection process for vacancies. As an applicant, you will interact with the front-end interface when you submit an application to a school, school district, or other organization that is managing the hiring process. At a minimum, you will provide answers to specific questions about your background and submit your resume through the ATS. Organizations may also ask you to provide writing samples, copies of certifications, transcripts, or take an online assessment, such as the Gallup TeacherInsight Assessment.

Recruiters, principals, and other hiring managers interact with the ATS on the back-end when they review your application and resume. They may also use functions of the ATS to manage lists of applications, enter hiring transactions, and generate communications to candidates at different stages in the process.

Every ATS is different. If you are applying to a large school district, they are likely using a highly-customized system with a sophisticated level of functionality that allows them to sort and filter through large numbers of resumes. You may also be applying to be included in a pool of candidates who will be considered for all jobs in a school district. If you are applying to a smaller organization, they may license a lower-cost off-the-shelf program that allows someone to evaluate applicants for one or two positions more efficiently than having candidates email their resumes directly to the principal.

So that's an ATS. Do I have to worry about this creature? Is it really as awful as my Google search results say?

While it's to your advantage to understand the basics of what an ATS does, you don't have to worry much about it. As an applicant, your responsibilities are to read all of the instructions on the application meticulously, follow them to the letter, and provide excellent materials.

Many applicants get held up when they fall prey to two ATS myths.

ATS myth one:
You need a special resume to apply for jobs via an ATS.

Recruiting organizations have used some version of an ATS for many years. Once upon a time, your average ATS had lousy functionality. Most of these then state-of-the-art systems couldn't accept attachments. The few that could take attachments required resumes to be basic, stripped-down files. You'll still find articles online that recommend you create a resume with little formatting and submit it via the ATS in Rich Text Format (RTF), as a Text file (TXT), or as a Microsoft Word document (DOC or DOCX).

This advice is mostly outdated. Today you'll most likely **submit a resume in Portable Document Format (PDF), which keeps the document formatted.** We'll discuss how to make a resume pretty and well formatted in Chapter Four.

You might face an instance where an ancient ATS system will only accept your file in RTF or DOC/DOCX format or ask you to copy and paste the text of your resume in an application field. **That is why it is your responsibility to read and follow all directions when applying for a job.** We will prepare you in advance for these rare cases in this chapter's exercises.

ATS myth two:
All ATS systems are designed to automatically scan resumes for keywords and eliminate as many resumes as possible before the recruitment process even begins.

Most organizations do NOT use their ATS to automatically screen resumes. Even when they do, this myth is an exaggeration. ATS screening is mostly used in other industries, such as technology, where jobs might require a very specific programming skill. Most educational institutions hand-screen resumes for many reasons, including that **they are looking for patterns in your resume that demonstrate potential,** something an automatic keyword assessment tool cannot do. We will discuss how to establish these patterns in Chapter Two and how to include basic keywords that are important for your teaching resume in Chapter Three.

Even in the worst-case, Jetsons-universe situation where a computer program does a significant first-review screening of applications based on keywords, think about what would happen if you made that cut. Your selected resume will be passed to a human being and a messy, cluttered, unformatted document of keywords that tells no story will not get you very far with him or her.

Write your resume with the end-goal of having a hiring manager run to the phone to schedule an interview with you.

Must I apply via the ATS or can I submit a paper copy of my resume directly to a school?

In 99.9% of all cases, you **must apply** via the ATS despite any contact you may have had with an organization's hiring representatives. There are many reasons why an organization needs standard information on everyone who is applying for a job, including government regulations on equity and open access. Also, the system streamlines the communication and hiring process for everyone involved. If you know you are going to speak with a principal about an opening, apply online with the organization via the ATS as soon as possible.

I know I am biased as a recruiter, but **I believe that you should appreciate the ATS as an applicant.** Here are three reasons to back that up:

- First, if a recruiter had to rely on a mountain of paper submissions or emails, that would be tough to organize and the hiring process would take forever. Trust me. I graduated college before people applied for jobs on the internet!

- Second, you might not be hired for the job you apply for, but a recruiter could search the list of applicants and call you for an even better job that just opened.

- Third, when you are hired, it often speeds up the payroll process because the organization already has critical employment information you submitted via the ATS. You will find that receiving your first paycheck on time is certainly helpful.

> **Successful resumes are designed for humans, not machines.**

What else do I need to know about the job search process beyond the ATS

Now that you know everything important about working with an ATS, let's continue talking about important principles for creating your resume and navigating the hiring process.

I mentioned this previously, but your goal is to impress real live people who are screening resumes and ultimately making hiring decisions. Even though we stressed all the reasons why submitting an excellent application via an ATS is necessary, it's not sufficient. Only a small percentage of you will be able to say in September that you were hired simply because you applied to an opening you found online. You must also get your resume out there to people in your network.

My third teacher recruiter confession: despite these fancy systems we use to keep track of the recruitment and hiring process, some teacher hiring happens offline and in very organic ways. Most recruiters won't tell you that, but it's true. A principal will meet an impressive aspiring teacher at church and then recommend her to a colleague to consider for an opening. An experienced teacher will refer a student teacher she is mentoring to the school where she started her career. While these matches are unexpected, they often end up being good ones.

To hook your dream job, you have to follow the official hiring guidelines and the unstated rules at the same time.

Let's consider some facts about networking and your resume.

Fact one:
Networking accounts for over two-thirds of hiring in almost every industry.

Your professional reputation and relationships matter. Most people will do business with someone they already know or someone recommended by someone they already know. Surveys consistently find that 60 to 80% of people who find jobs do so through networking. This is certainly true in teaching where principals are community leaders and meet people through all aspects of their lives.

If you're spending all of your time updating your resume to make it a monster document of keywords for your next submission to an ATS, and there is only a 20% chance you're going to get a job through applying online... well, you can do the math and figure out the probability of success. Maybe it's time to switch up how you spend your time?

Fact two:
You'll likely be hired through networking, but not by someone you already know.

Mark Granovetter, an accomplished and brilliant Stanford-based sociologist, has spent most of his career studying social networks. He found that the most influential part of our network is our weak ties, people who are second or third degree connections from our direct contacts. This is very important in the marketing field, and for the dissemination of information, but it is also critical to your job search.

It's more likely you'll be considered for jobs by colleagues or associates of someone you know rather than a close connection. That means your resume will be passed on to a principal by a neighbor or someone who belongs to the same civic association as you. This second degree connection will value the initial recommendation, but learn about you from your resume.

The clear and concise resume encourages the principal who hasn't met you yet to give you a call. **The cluttered and mediocre resume gets thrown in the trash.**

Tracy's Tip!

Here's another interesting fact about networking and the job search: Granovetter found that the larger a person's network, the more career success that person achieved, especially as measured by income. Sometimes dusting off your party shoes and hitting some events to meet new people is the best career move you can make. You may end up with many unexpected people to email your resume to the next day.

So you're saying DON'T create customized resumes for every position? I've heard different advice.

The goal of this book is to help you create an extraordinary resume that works in the majority of situations. A PDF of your one extraordinary resume can be quickly forwarded the next day to the teacher you had a great conversation with at a party who told you that she thinks her principal may have an opening. In a scenario where you have all the time and energy in the world, it may be a great strategy to customize your resume for each of the 25 jobs you'll apply for in one hiring season. But since you don't, you have to make choices about what you do with your time. You'll be better off spending more time networking and researching schools than customizing a resume over and over again.

Once you have an extraordinary resume, you can certainly make some slight adjustments for positions and schools you're really interested in by swapping some accomplishments and referring to your keyword bank, especially in your cover letter. Just don't stress about it or make customization your primary focus. I've included more information on creating a keyword bank in Chapter Three and review cover letters in Chapter Five.

Okay. I am convinced that I need a resume for humans. Who is going to read my resume during the hiring process? Any tips for communicating with these people?

Who reviews your resume depends on the organization. If you are applying to a large school district, a professional screener may first screen your resume before it is passed to a recruiter. If you are applying to a small school, a school aide could do the first review. He or she might check for grammar and basic experience and forward the favorites to the principal or hiring committee.

When I open a resume, I make a decision if it can easily be scanned. If yes, I scan it for 10-20 seconds, looking for patterns and skills (discussed in Chapter Two) and to ensure the person writes well and organizes information effectively (discussed in Chapter Four).

Who specifically reviews your resume is less important than understanding that they are all looking for excellence in your past accomplishments and the potential to change their students' futures.

When communicating with anyone about your job search, keep your communication absolutely formal. I advise not writing to principals and recruiters via your mobile devices unless you promise to check every typo and maintain the formality you would use if you were typing with a full screen and keyboard. Sometimes I receive emails from applicants who treat me with the same level of respect they'd offer a debt collector, or the messages are filled with iPhone autocorrect abbreviations that my old person's brain doesn't understand. **I reply back to those emails saying that all of my interview slots have been filled.**

Final questions about the process: why does teacher hiring take so darn long, and when should I start applying?

Oh yes. It is true—the teacher hiring process often takes months, even at the most organized charter schools with few positions to fill. There are lots of factors that influence the length of the process. For starters...

- Administrators often receive school budgets later than desired, which is outside their control. Local governments that fund school districts and charter schools have to make difficult decisions on how to use a finite amount of tax dollars and that process can take time.

- Currently employed teachers may need additional time to determine what they are going to do next year, such as applying for a promotion at another school or moving away to be closer to family. Many openings surface when those decisions are made in late spring/early summer.

- Finally, school administrators wear many hats and the hiring hat is only one of them. If a job posting attracts hundreds of resumes, it takes more time at every stage. Principals do the best they can to prioritize the tasks they have in any given day and sometimes hiring is the task they choose to delay. **Your sense of urgency is not always shared.**

You should still apply as early in the hiring season as possible. Research conducted in 2003 by TNTP, a teacher research organization, found that despite the late hiring, teachers who applied early were more successful in their job search than those who waited. Often, I will have an unexpected opening pop-up in August and go back to stellar resumes I received in April. **Early resumes are the ones we remember.**

Alright! You should now feel as if you have a good understanding of how the teacher hiring process works, how your resume is viewed at every stage of the recruitment process, and what is expected of you. The following exercises for Chapter One will help you develop systems that will save you a significant amount of time throughout your job search.

CHAPTER ONE EXERCISES

Task	Done? Check off enthusiastically once the answer is yes!
1. Create file storage and note-taking systems.	

First, decide where you will store multiple versions of your resume. I recommend storing your important documents in the cloud so your documents are secure, backed up, and accessible anywhere. I am a fan of Dropbox, but you may be more comfortable with Google Drive or another service.

If you use Dropbox, I recommend creating a folder called "Resume," and a subfolder within it called "Old Resumes." When you make updates to the Microsoft Word version of your resume (DOC/DOCX), create a new file and move any older versions into the subfolder.

You will also need a place to keep online notes for your resume and cover letter. This may be a file in Dropbox, Google Drive, or a notebook in Evernote, my favorite note-taking tool. You will want to cut and paste information that you decide to edit out of your current version, but may want to reconsider in a future resume if your goals change. You will also want to create a note for keywords and one for common sentences you use in your cover letters. We'll talk more about keywords in Chapter Three and cover letters in Chapter Five.

Task	Done? Check off enthusiastically once the answer is yes!
2. Create DOC/DOCX, TXT, RTF, and PDF versions of your current resume.	

Use the Microsoft Word (DOC/DOCX) version of your resume as your base resume. Every time you make revisions save a Rich Text Format (RTF), Text (TXT), and Portable

Document File (PDF) version of your resume as well. In addition to the DOC/DOCX version of your resume, your "Resume" folder should hold these three versions at all times. Here's why:

- The RTF version of your resume is used when an Application Tracking System specifically asks for you to submit your resume as an RTF file. In Microsoft Word, choose Save As from the File menu and change the Format option to Rich Text Format (RTF).

- The TXT version of your resume is used when an Application Tracking System specifically asks for you to copy and paste the text of your resume in a field on the application. TXT removes formatting tags that will make text copied and pasted from DOC/DOCX or RTF files appear strange when it is submitted. In Microsoft Word, choose Save As from the File menu and change the Format option to Text (TXT).

- **The PDF version of your resume is used almost every time you submit your application because it maintains your formatting.** In Microsoft Word, choose Save As from the File menu and change the Format option to Portable Document Format (PDF).

Whenever you make edits to your resume, only make edits to the Microsoft Word version and then save copies in the other three recommended formats.

Task	Done? Check off enthusiastically once the answer is yes!
3. Adopt a naming convention for your resume that guarantees it is opened.	

When I am doing a teacher search, I often download 10-20 resumes from the ATS onto my desktop. **If a file name does not have the applicant's name in it, I can't remember why I have the file and often trash it.**

Name the current PDF version of your resume "First Name Last Name Resume." For example, simply name the file "Joe Smith Resume" if your name is Joe Smith. **Do not include version numbers or dates in the file name. These details can be confusing to everyone but you.**

Before making edits to a resume file, make a copy of your current DOC/DOCX file and add the current date to the end before you store it in your "Old Resume" folder. You can delete other outdated RTF, TXT and PDF versions of your resume.

Task	Done? Check off enthusiastically once the answer is yes!
4. Implement a journaling tool.	

Your professional journey is just beginning. If you don't currently journal, you should start so you can record the victories, as well as the less stellar moments from your teaching career, that you'll want to add to your resume, talk about in an interview, or even present on some day. According to *The Harvard Business Review*, "keeping a journal is one of the best strategies for learning about yourself and improving your professional performance over time."

While many people prefer paper journals, I highly recommend **OhLife.com.** OhLife.com sends you a daily email asking you how your day was and you log your daily reflection by replying to the email. You can also attach pictures. Your entries are stored securely in the cloud and you can view and export them at any time. A premium account will also allow you the ability to search all your entries for specific terms. I have used OhLife.com for three years and have never missed an entry!

CHAPTER TWO: DIFFERENTIATING YOURSELF FROM YOUR PEERS

Last year, I read *The Start-up of You: Adapt to the Future, Invest in Yourself, and Transform Your Career* by Reid Hoffman, a founder of LinkedIn. I highly recommend it. Hoffman speaks about the habits of successful professionals, including how they differentiate and market their "assets," or their strengths and value to a potential client or employer. In one of his presentations on the book, he said that we need to keep this in mind "whether you are a lawyer or doctor or teacher or engineer or even a business owner."

Even I was initially taken aback by how he included teachers in his statement about marketing yourself, but it's true. The days where you could get a teaching job because you were certified, cared about kids, and were basically mentally sane are over. **Teachers must learn to talk about how they are different from their peers, even in the earliest days of their career.**

After finishing the book, I reflected on the traditionally prepared student teachers I've worked with who never understand why they are passed over for positions in favor of candidates from Teach For America or similar alternative certification programs. After all, student teachers have more training, right? Maybe, but have they truly expressed what they accomplished during that training so that it matters? Teachers from special programs have been trained to tell principals about themselves in compelling ways, and, more specifically, how those experiences have made them better equipped to change kids' lives.

Recruiters and principals—real people like you—enjoy interesting, well-told stories that highlight human potential.

How do you make a resume interesting?

Brooke Allen, a financial services professional I respect and admire, frequently gives free talks around New York City to the unemployed. According to Allen, there are only two things you need to write a good resume: (1) do interesting stuff and (2) know how to write well.

I could not summarize this better.

I know many recruiters and hiring managers who hate looking at resumes. I am not one of those people. It's not cool to confess this, but I find resumes fascinating because they tell unique stories about the many paths a person can take with their life. I especially love seeing what led career changers to teaching via their resume path. For me, a comfy chair, some locally roasted coffee, and a stack of good resumes isn't the worst way to spend a few hours.

This chapter is about how you can make your resume tell a story that's worthy of my comfy chair and beverage. **In other words, this chapter is about how to identify all of your interesting "stuff."**

> # An extraordinary resume tells a unique and overarching story of excellence.

Successful people think about their resume as a great piece of content that has a purpose and tells a story. **A well-written resume allows the reviewer to get a feel for what you strive for, what you value, and your past decision-making patterns.**

Mediocre resumes fail to reveal this information.

Here's my fourth teacher recruiter confession: a few years ago, my team attended a teacher recruitment fair at a hotel in Pennsylvania, sponsored by a major university. We met hundreds of teachers who handed us their resumes, hoping to be considered for our job openings. As the team packed up our leftover recruitment swag at the end of the day, we skimmed through the resumes. Over 80% of the resumes followed a (badly formatted) template, likely developed by the career center. Every one of those students described their student teaching with these same three bullets:

- Assisted cooperating teacher
- Developed lesson plans
- Managed student discipline issues

None of those students took the effort to customize the template and tell a story that was unique to their experience and accomplishments. **We threw out all the resumes before we left the hotel.**

What do principals and schools want in new team members?

As a teacher recruiter, I look for resume patterns that demonstrate potential skills and how the applicant might fit with a particular school, job, and/or a principal. I also want to hire people who are likeable and have a strong work ethic, but those are things I measure in an interview and not in a document.

New teachers and career changers have not had a chance to demonstrate that they are excellent teachers yet. However, economists have found there are some basic skills and behaviors successful people possess that can be assessed via professional achievements. These are often called **transferable skills** because they transfer across jobs, industries, and academic experiences. I look for the following transferable skills when I evaluate new teachers' resumes.

- Being accountable to your own goals
- Demonstrating intellectual curiosity
- Taking advantage of leadership opportunities
- Pursuing challenges and taking risks
- Achieving goals with children (if applicable)

Overall, extraordinary resumes explain how the applicant achieved measurable results in all these areas. Extraordinary resumes also display excellent communication and organization skills, but we'll talk about that more in Chapters Three and Four, respectively.

What have you accomplished or participated in thus far in your academic and professional career that align with these skills and habits?

If you are an experienced teacher, I am looking for everything I've described above and for what you have accomplished with students. Your resume story must answer the following two questions above all else:

- How have the students you've worked with grown, both on achievement tests and in other inspiring ways?

- How have you been an instructional leader in your school or district?

Along with these skills and behaviors, I look for other patterns and specific activities that would appeal to a specific principal. For example, are you also an artist? Have you worked in small or big organizations your entire life? This helps with the specific matching process with schools and principals.

How can I create great resume stories?

A story is demonstrated through a pattern of activities and experiences that emphasize the biggest strengths you have to offer as a job applicant.

Below are examples of common stories of achieving results through using transferable skills that can be reflected in a resume. All of these stories can be told by experienced career changers and young professionals who have actively participated in campus life and had internships or part-time jobs.

SKILL OR BEHAVIOR	HOW AN EXTRAORDINARY RESUME PORTRAYS THIS STORY
Being accountable to your own goals	• Consistent measurable results listed for all work experiences • Academic achievement
Demonstrating intellectual curiosity	• Continued education • Presentations and facilitations • Participation in a variety of activities and groups outside the classroom • Shared expertise with others both formally and informally
Taking advantage of leadership opportunities	• Formal promotions and leadership positions at work and in clubs • Increased responsibility within a company or job

Pursuing challenges and risks	• Problem/solution approach to describing your accomplishments • Launching new programs and groups • Turning around programs and projects • Studying abroad
Achieving goals with children (if applicable)	• Student progress on formal or informal learning goals and projects • Successful and inspiring lessons and units

While everyone will have stories to show how they possess these skills and behaviors, every story will be different. The strengths gained from these experiences and how they will inform the work at a new school should be described in a unique way. **This differentiation is what will make a resume stand out.**

Tracy's Tip!

The stories you compile as part of these exercises should also inform your job search. If you're someone who likes to start new things, it's likely you're going to hit walls at a traditional large school with an experienced faculty set in their ways. If you like order, the up and down start-up culture of the typical new school will make you crazy.

Most people who seek to change their job due to dissatisfaction admit that they saw warning signs during their job search. Pay attention to these signals to maximize your fit with a school and manager.

Here are exercises to help you think about how you will tell compelling stories through your resume.

CHAPTER TWO EXERCISES

Task	Done? Check off enthusiastically once the answer is yes!
1. Review your current resume and brainstorm stories that demonstrate desired skills and behaviors.	

List stories for each of the skills and behaviors recruiters are looking for in new teachers. If you can, show that you demonstrated success in the following areas with students.

- Being accountable to your own goals
- Demonstrating intellectual curiosity
- Taking advantage of leadership opportunities
- Pursuing challenges and taking risks
- Achieving goals with children (if applicable)

Many of the overachievers reading this have already decided that their resume is going to reflect every story that could possibly illustrate an intellectually curious risk-taking leader. Stop. While it's great to include everything you can think of during a brainstorming session, you'll need to focus on the top few stories for your resume. When you're done brainstorming, rank your stories in order of importance. **In fact, start ranking them now.**

Task	Done? Check off enthusiastically once the answer is yes!
2. List the most important details that support your story.	

A good storyteller can tell his or her story concisely and without every detail. We'll talk about this in detail in Chapter Three and I'll teach you how to convert details into effective accomplishment bullets. When creating your resume, remember it is the document you use to get an interview and much should be left for that event.

Many details about your positions can be left out and discussed one-on-one with the recruiter or hiring manager.

Task	Done? Check off enthusiastically once the answer is yes!
3. Ask a friend or mentor to read your resume and tell you what stories it tells.	

A good way to know if you are telling an authentic story is to ask people who know you to review your resume and tell you if it represents how they see you as a professional. **Do they feel it demonstrates your important transferable skills?**

As an additional exercise, email your friends and family to send back three words that describe your best skills as a professional. I did this exercise when I launched my business, and I realized I was downplaying some of my greatest strengths.

Task	Done? Check off enthusiastically once the answer is yes!
4. Review your resume with a fresh perspective.	

Before we transition to Chapter Three on creating your resume step-by-step, pull out your current resume and ask yourself the following questions:

- Does this look like something I'd want to read if I was hiring someone? Does it look clear and interesting? If the answer is no, we'll teach you how to fix this in Chapter Four.

- Is there superfluous and repetitive information hanging around your resume from when you submitted your resume for a previous position? If yes, highlight those items or delete them. You can cut and paste keywords or phrases into the note-taking system you created in Chapter One.

Now that we've touched on identifying your "interesting stuff," Chapters Three and Four talk about how to write about it well. Let's move on!

CHAPTER THREE: CREATING YOUR EXTRAORDINARY RESUME SECTION BY SECTION

We're now into the nitty-gritty of this book—how to create an extraordinary resume that prompts someone to call you for an interview immediately.

If you skipped Chapters One and Two because you're one of those people who like to get to the point... fine! But remember that your resume will only be mediocre if you haven't thought through all the questions and completed all the exercises presented previously, so please go back and review them at your earliest convenience.

> **An extraordinary resume is comprised of extraordinary details.**

In the last chapter, we defined your overarching story of accountability, leadership, curiosity, and results. Now we'll go section by section through an extraordinary resume and fill in the details. This will be helpful for you regardless of whether you are a recent graduate, career changer, or experienced teacher.

Resume Sections You Need

- Contact Information
- Summary Statement (optional)
- Education
- Certifications
- Experience(s)
- The Catch-all Section(s): Leadership, Skills, and Affiliations

Tracy's Tip!

While we will talk more about formatting in Chapter Four, keep in mind as you work through the sections that **we are aiming to create a resume that fits on one page** for anyone with less than ten years of experience or significant academic work. If you are more experienced, you can plan for two pages. A resume includes your key story and supporting details, not everything you have ever done or topics that are better discussed in an interview. A recruiter **will not read** a resume that is too long.

Also, an extraordinary resume lists your education and experience in reverse chronological order. You may have heard of functional resumes that group all your skills by competency at the beginning of your resume. Like most recruiters, **I believe functional resumes are evil.** They are impossible to scan, so I close them and move on. I only trust that you have the skills you say if they are embedded within your work history.

Contact Information

Include your contact information in the header of your document to save space. This section should include a current mailing address, phone number, email, and link to a web presence. Some notes about your contact information:

- It is unlikely that anyone is going to send you physical mail through the job search, but you must still include a mailing address. If you are living at college, you can add a current address and permanent address. However, listing only one address is preferable. If you do list a current address, include the date you expect to move.

- Only include one phone number, preferably your cell.

- We will talk about web presence and digital portfolios in Chapter Six, but it is a great idea to include a link to your LinkedIn profile or digital portfolio.

Tracy's Tip!

I have very specific advice about what type of email address to include on a resume: get a Gmail address with a professional handle. For some reason, out of everything I talk about regarding resumes in my career coaching workshops with teachers, this recommendation gets them riled up the most!

As I discussed in the Introduction, you are free to discard advice that you don't feel applies to you, but here are the reasons why I make this Gmail recommendation.

- **Your email handle should be a simple variation of your name.** Try to avoid numbers unless you have a very common name and it's unavoidable. It's 2013, but I still get resumes from the strangest email addresses. I once received a resume from Donald Duck <mightymouse@xxxxx.com>. One cartoon character is bad enough, but why did the person choose two? I'll never know.

- **Email domains have certain stigmas that are then applied to people who use them.** You can Google "what your email address says about your computer skills" to get a sense of that. Gmail users are generally perceived as more professional and educated than those who use other services to manage their email. **People will judge you for your Yahoo or (gasp!) AOL email address.** Technology skills are important for teachers, so why make a principal wonder if you are tech savvy from the start?

- **There is evidence that job applicants who use Gmail addresses on their resumes are more successful.** A 2009 study found that job applicants with Gmail addresses were 40% more likely to be contacted by recruiters than applicants with other addresses.

- **I do not contact people who provide an email with an .edu domain.** While college policies have changed, universities used to delete new graduates' email accounts within days of graduation. When a vacancy opens in August and I have a quick window to fill it, I go through my hot resumes, often considering resumes I received in the spring. Too often I would email a promising new graduate at their .edu address and have the email bounce back. Now if I see an .edu email address on a resume, I assume I will not be able to get in touch with the person easily and try to find someone else with better contact information.

Summary Statement (optional)

Experienced professionals may decide to start their resumes with a simple summary statement that provides an overview of who they are within the context of their job search.

Summary statements do not have to be fancy. Here are some examples for each job seeker category.

If you are an experienced teacher, your summary statement should be about student results. I will search for supporting details within your experience section.

Veteran science teacher with 10 years of experience leading students toward high levels of achievement.

If you are a career changer, your summary statement should start with a description of who you are now and include how your previous experience will help you achieve your teaching goals.

Newly certified math teacher dedicated to using my experience in the engineering industry to inspire and help students achieve success in the STEM field.

If you are a new graduate, focus on your goals.

Newly certified English teacher committed to motivating my students to love knowledge and think critically throughout their academic careers.

LinkedIn publishes an annual report listing the most overused words and phrases on profiles, including "track record," "dynamic," and "results-oriented," words often found in summary statements. Every year this press release spawns a million blog posts saying that you should never use these words. A million job seekers then spend hours combing the thesaurus for exotic adjectives to include in their resume.

While you want the language on your resume to stand out, the truth is that there is a language for resumes and some phrases like "track record" will often appear, and that's okay. The real question is if you do use one of these terms, do you have the work experience to back it up?

- If you say you have a "track record" or "extensive experience in a field," I expect to see ten years of significant accomplishments throughout the rest of your resume.

- If you say you are "innovative" or "results-oriented," I expect to see quantified results that show this.

- If you say you're "dynamic," "motivated," or a "team-player," I'll gloss over that information because I think it's impossible to prove it on a resume. Those are traits of a person, not results. Skip these terms on your resume. I'll figure out if you have these qualities in an interview.

Again, summary statements are optional and generally used by more experienced professionals.

Tracy's Tip!

There is definitely one section I don't want to see on your resume and that is the objective section. Recruiters don't like objectives on resumes. There are a few dissenters, but it's not a best practice. Here are four reasons why it's a good idea to leave an objective off your resume.

- **I know your objective because you have submitted an application to a job I posted.** Your objective is taking up space and limiting how much you can talk about all the amazing things you've done, which is what I really want to know about at this stage of the process.

- **Objectives are incredibly hard to write.** It is difficult to use proper grammar with any sentence that starts with "To." Why should awkward language be the first impression you make?

- **Your goal is to position yourself as a candidate who is going to add tremendous value to a school above all else.** If the first thing I read is about all the things you want in your objective—a supportive environment with strict discipline policies and excellent professional development—it makes me pause. Those are not ridiculous things to want as a new teacher, or for a school to provide, but you must give before you ask as a jobseeker. Reading an objective that lists all your demands makes me subconsciously wonder if you are going to always be asking for things and whether you are going to be the tenacious and constant learner I need for my students.

- **Motivations are assessed in an interview or cover letter, not a resume.** This is an important rule: never include content on a resume that is not specifically tied to tangible accomplishments I can verify. I'll want to learn why you want to be a teacher, but not here. The soft stuff is for the interview stage.

Education

If you are an experienced teacher, the education section of your resume should follow the experience section(s). For recent graduates and career changers, you should list your education at the beginning or right under your summary statement if you choose to use one.

Unqualified people submit resumes for teaching jobs all the time. Listing your degree from a teacher preparation program at the top is a signal that you are qualified and I'll keep reading.

Here are the rules for describing your education on your resume.

- Educational experiences are listed in reverse chronological order. Your most recent experience comes first, even if the degree is in progress.

- List the full name of every school you attended and include its city and state. If applicable, include the college at the university if it has its own name.

- List the degree you received or will receive with the graduation date. If you have not yet received a degree, identify it as anticipated.

- Include your major and any honors or activities that were specific to your academic experience.

Here is an example of how a new teacher in a master's program might list his education on his resume.

New York University New York, NY
The Steinhardt School of Culture, Education and Human Development
Master of Education, Anticipated May 2013, GPA 3.5
Major: Childhood Education
Honors: Awesome Teaching Fellowship

University of Michigan Ann Arbor, MI
The Gerald R. Ford School of Public Policy
Bachelor of Arts, May 2011
Major: Public Policy
Honors and Activities: Chancellor's Scholar, Global Intercultural Experience Program in Argentina (2010)

MORE EDUCATION SECTION RULES

- If you are currently in school, include your GPA (if it is over 3.0), and, if you made the dean's list, state that you made the dean's list. **If you have graduated, do not include your GPA or the fact that you were on the dean's list.** These are achievements that are less relevant after you've graduated. Once you have graduated, the only honors that are noteworthy on a resume are Latin honors: *cum laude* (honor), *magna cum laude* (great honor), or *summa cum laude* (highest honor). Consult with your university to find out their requirements for awarding these distinctions.

- Honors and activities listed in the education section are directly tied to your academics. These are different than awards you may have earned in other areas of your life; those belong in the leadership section, discussed later in this chapter. **If you received a fellowship to become a teacher through a preparation program associated with your university, you would list it in the education section.** Achievements should only be listed once on your resume, so don't include information about your fellowship here AND in your leadership section.

- Principals love teachers who studied abroad, and the education section is the place to mention these experiences. Principals believe an experience abroad shows that you take risks and are likely cultural sensitive. If you are working in an underserved community, many of your students may have never traveled and your experiences can inspire them to go abroad when they reach college.

- If you have a degree that resulted in academic publications, you should list them in this section under the associated university.

Certification

It is important to list the teacher certifications you have on your resume clearly and correctly. Some school districts and states have very specific rules about which certifications can be used for which position, meaning not every math certification qualifies you for every math teacher vacancy.

If you are a new graduate or a career changer, your certification section should follow your education near the beginning of your resume, unless you are a career changer who became certified outside of an institution of higher education. In that case, list your certification before your education as a signal that you are qualified. If you are an experienced teacher, certification can appear as one of the final sections of your resume.

For each certification, list the legal name of your certificate and the state. If your certification has not yet been issued because you are still completing your requirements, list the anticipated date.

Here are two examples:

- Certificate of Eligibility in Biological Science, New Jersey, Anticipated September 2013

- Single Subject Teaching Certificate in Mathematics, California

MORE CERTIFICATION SECTION RULES

- Do not list expired certificates. If you want to list it on your resume, renew it first.

- Whatever you list on your resume, make sure that you take care of all application requirements for certification early in the recruitment process. I have recruited amazing new graduates who I had to send packing the week before school started because they waited until the last minute to send in their certification application, and it was not going to be reviewed by the state education department before the first day of school. It is illegal in most states to hire uncertified teachers.

Experience Section(s)

Your experience is what demonstrates you are a truly extraordinary professional. Let's talk about how to structure this part of your resume.

You may decide to have more than one experience section if you are a new teacher or career changer. You can use a "teaching experience" section that details your student teaching and other school experience and an "other professional experience" section to highlight your other work. It is not necessary to structure your resume this way, but it is a good option if you have had lots of other experiences before you began this career.

Your non-teaching experience matters. This may be obvious for career changers, but not as much for recent graduates. A few years ago, I noticed a phenomenon where many of the new graduates from a top New York City university, one where students pay a lot of money for tuition, would only list their student teaching experience on their resumes and no other work experience. We found out from the students that their career center told them that non-teaching experience was irrelevant and to eliminate everything else that was not associated with their university work.

Worst. Resume. Advice. Ever.

First, common sense should indicate that having one experience on your resume creates a lopsided document. This is not how you want your resume to stand out in a pile! Second, as we discussed in Chapter Two, I want to hire teachers who demonstrate they can manage multiple responsibilities, are leaders, and are engaged in varied activities. If you did nothing but show up to your student teaching and study, why would I think you are someone who would inspire my students? Your part-time job working at the school library is important because it allowed you to develop leadership skills, among others.

You do not have to list every job you ever had. If you have been in the workforce for some time or have experiences you don't believe need to be highlighted, you can list your job accomplishments in one summary bullet point. For example, if you were an entry-level researcher five years ago and you now have more advanced accomplishments, you may summarize that early experience in one umbrella bullet.

- Contributed research to 6 food science studies that influenced FDA regulations on poultry.

You do not have to list detailed accomplishments. If I am curious and want to learn more, I'll ask in an interview.

If you've been out of school more than one year, limit how many collegiate experiences you include. When I transitioned from college to being an adult worker 15ish years ago, I struggled with letting go of my college experiences, both on paper and in my mind. I was Queen Bee in college. I completed four internships and had helped direct sorority rush for 600 freshman girls (an experience that certainly influenced my attraction to recruitment). However, by the time I was two years out of college, I was an adult with more relevant experiences and was struggling with keeping my resume to one page. I felt like I was letting go of my identity when I hit the delete button on all that college experience, but realized the leadership activities that had defined me at age 21 weren't the ones I needed to excel at age 24. I needed to accept that and move forward.

Tracy's Tip!

Most recent graduates and career changers get tripped up on how to talk about their student teaching and observation experiences effectively on their resume. In Chapter Two I confessed how my team discarded close to 100 resumes from teachers who cut and paste the same three bullets from a resume template. This lack of description of the student teaching experience is actually widespread for new teachers, and it's critical you don't make the same mistake as those students and miss your opportunity. Here are a few more tips that will help you create a stand-out description of your student teaching experience.

- **Student teaching is a job, and it belongs in your experience section.** You may not have earned money as a student teacher, but your responsibilities were of a job nature and you were assessed as an employee. You can also list any observation experiences that you had in schools if you interacted with students and had specific duties.

- **You need to tell me what you specifically accomplished in your student teaching.** This is not the place to be humble. I know that you had tangible results with your students and can tell me about your potential. Here are a few questions to ask yourself to help frame your experience in terms of results:

    1. How many students did you teach and what grades?
    2. Did you complete a full unit with your students? What was the title of your most successful lesson? How did you know the unit or lesson was successful for your students?
    3. Did your students take any formal or informal assessments while you were student teaching? How much progress did your students make?
    4. Were there any special events that you took a leadership role in (e.g., science fair)?

- **Let me reiterate that it's about student-centered results and not the tasks of teaching.** I do not want to see "developed lesson plans" as a bullet point on your resume. All student teachers develop lesson plans. I want to know about your successful lesson and its impact on your students. I bet you did something really cool that made your students get excited about learning. Tell me about it on your resume.

- **Finally, you need to write about your student teaching accomplishments and not your cooperating teacher's.** I should also never read the words "cooperating teacher" on a resume. Listing an experience as student teaching implies you were not alone in the classroom. I want to know what you did with your students when you were in charge.

As you draft your experience section, remember the goal is to tell the story of how you became a high performer, not create a laundry list of individual achievements.

Rules for Describing Your Accomplishments

Format is important. Your experiences are listed in reverse chronological order, just as in the education section. Specific accomplishments are written in bullet point format, not full-sentences.

Each experience you list on your resume consists of a job title, company, location, dates, and **bulleted accomplishment statements.** Extraordinary resumes do not talk about job duties, but accomplishments. I want to know what you did in the job, not what the expectations were of you.

Each experience will have between one-to-five accomplishment bullet points to support it. Experiences with five accomplishment bullets are significant ones, meaning you managed large teams and achieved high-impact results. Your first bullet should be an umbrella accomplishment of what you did in this position, with the other bullets being about more specific accomplishments. For example, your bullet that states you were a teacher who taught calculus to 100+ students would precede your bullet about advising the 20-member math club after school.

You may be confused about the difference between job duties and accomplishments on a resume. To illustrate the difference, here are experience section examples from two recent graduates who attended the same university and had similar jobs during college.

Applicant One:

Graduate Assistant   01/10-05/13
Office of Parent and Family Programs, XXX University   New York, NY
- Communicated with parents
- Diffused crisis situations
- Planned campus-wide events in support of the program director

Applicant Two:

Graduate Assistant   01/10-05/13
Department of Residential Programs, XXX University   New York, NY
- Served as a mentor, leader, and a 24/7 multi-purpose resource for 30-45 resident advisors
- Ensured a safe, fun, and comfortable living and learning experience for all students
- Programmed 5 unique social and community building events for resident advisor community

The first applicant talks about her experience in terms of her job duties, while the second applicant describes her accomplishments. You can see that the accomplishments example stands out. I have no idea what the first student did. Is diffusing a crisis situation simply negotiating an argument between two students or something more significant with dozens of people? What were her responsibilities in regards to the campus-wide events other than to stand behind the program director?

> ### Tracy's Tip!
>
> **Career changers: You do not need to write a description of your past companies.** Anything that the recruiter needs to know will be reflected in the accomplishment bullet. If the recruiter has questions, he or she will follow-up in an interview.
>
> Job titles are listed before your company on resumes because what you did is always more important than where you did it.

Each accomplishment bullet is written in parallel structure. This means it starts with an action verb and includes a metric or result and context, if needed. One of the most important rules of resumes is to **never, ever write a bullet point in your experience section that does not start with an action verb!**

Each accomplishment statement should be quantified. You want to measure what you accomplished with numbers whenever possible. On resumes, you should write every number in its numerical form, no matter how small (i.e., 5 instead of five). Numbers stand out on a resume by breaking up the text and by making the person scanning your resume slow down and engage in what you've written.

More importantly, quantified results show that you can actually do everything you say you can.

The following is an example of how someone might quantify his student teaching experiences. Note how every bullet point begins with an action verb and ends with the results. Also, remember that because he has listed his position as "Student Teacher," this applicant does not need to mention his cooperating teacher in his accomplishments. It is implied that other people helped him or participated in these achievements based on the title. What is important is that the applicant took an active role in achieving these results in his role as a student teacher.

Student Teacher   09/12–12/12
The Justin Timberlake Elementary School   Savannah, GA

- Taught 35 fourth graders through student-centered lessons and created a safe, organized, and positive classroom environment
- Led 95% of students to achieve a B+ or better on an interdisciplinary unit on women's history
- Coached winner of the school district spelling bee
- Participated in 3 school study teams on the Common Core standards

Almost every accomplishment bullet can be quantified in some way. Here are some other ways you can quantify what you accomplished.

- **Scale:** Sometimes our jobs impact a lot of people. When you say you handled accounts at a job before you began teaching, does that mean you handled one or 40 or 400? It matters! And how important were these accounts for the company?

- **Another example of scale:** if you indicate you "tutored students after school," I am wondering what that experience was like.
  Tutoring could mean sitting across from one student once a week and talking about reality television. If you write that you "Helped 13 struggling students read at grade level through interventions, tutoring, and coaching," I know what you did.

- **Increases or decreases:** Did you increase or decrease something important for an organization or students? Maybe you helped administer a program that decreased absences at your school?

- **Saving:** If you have office experience, it is likely you were tasked with doing something more efficiently, such as saving time or money. Tell me about it.

Now that we've drafted your parallel accomplishment bullets with action verbs and quantified results, let's discuss some other ways to spruce up your experience section(s).

Include keywords. I want you to be as organic as possible in how you describe your experience with students. If something is not authentic to your experience, you should not include a keyword because you believe you have to do so. However, here are common keywords that recruiters like to see on teacher resumes.

- Scaffolding
- Integrating
- Differentiating instruction
- Student-centered learning
- Direct instruction
- Learning styles
- Interdisciplinary units or lessons
- Classroom management
- Student engagement
- Parent involvement
- Data-driven instruction
- Assessment
- Research-based teaching
- Curriculum

A few more quick notes about using education keywords...

- **Data and assessment are sexy.** If you have worked with standardized test data or have previous experience working with data in your pre-teaching life, include it in your resume.

- If you have had **experiences with special needs or gifted and talented students** and accommodating instruction for them, definitely mention that, even if you are not a special education teacher.

- This bears repeating: **if you are an experienced teacher, you must quantify how your students grew under your leadership.** If you cannot use standardized test data, develop a list of other data points that demonstrate you positively impacted their achievement.

- Take note of common **keywords that show up frequently on teacher job postings** and find ways to include them if they are relevant to your experience.

Tracy's Tip!

Create a keyword bank. You may have words in your resume that aren't key to your current purpose, but you don't want to forget a term in case it becomes relevant for a specific occasion. For example, working with specific technology skills may not be relevant for most math positions. However, you could find that a school wants a teacher who also knows Photoshop to lead an afterschool club and you now want to highlight that you have that skill. Create a keyword bank that you can pull relevant words and phrases from in the future.

MORE EXPERIENCE SECTION RULES

- **Be clear, concise, and specific.** Be relentless in editing extraneous words. When it makes sense, use proper names of anything you can. For example, name the awesome unit you completed with your students instead of just referencing the subject.

- **Eliminate redundancy.** When we are evaluating your resume, we are looking for breadth of experiences and depth of accomplishments. If you answered phones at multiple jobs, you only have to list that accomplishment bullet once in your resume. If you mastered a skill at one job, you do not need to list that again in your older experiences.

- **Be consistent.** I do not use bullets after my accomplishment statements, but the more important lesson is to be consistent in how you use punctuation across experiences and sections. Remember to also be consistent how you use verb tenses. If you have finished your responsibilities at a position, the verb must be in the past tense. If you are still actively engaged in the activity or job, use the present tense.

- **Diversify verbs.** It's boring to read "managed" and "handled" ten times on your resume. Use a thesaurus to consider other verbs. Like adjectives, there is a fine line between making it interesting and producing giggles. For example, it's okay to say that you "Presented to a 100-person audience." If you say that you "Captivated a 100-person audience," you sound more interesting, but also like a magician. Giggle.

- **Avoid industry jargon.** You never know who will be reading your resume. A school's hiring committee could be very diverse and include parents and less senior school employees. Would someone who didn't know much about your background understand what you are saying about any non-teaching jobs?

- **Never write an accomplishment bullet that I couldn't theoretically verify.** Resumes are about definable accomplishments. Everything else, including interpersonal skills, is addressed in the interview.

The Catch-all Section(s): Leadership, Skills, and Affiliation Sections

Every resume should have **at least one** of the following three sections: **leadership, skills,** or **affiliations.** However, most of you will find it easier to have one catch-all section called **leadership, skills, and affiliations.** If you are a recent graduate, you may have only one or two bullet points between these three categories making it perfectly okay to combine them into one section. Experienced teachers and career changers may be struggling with page length requirements based on all the amazing accomplishments filling up your experience section(s). Combining these sections is an easy solution for saving space.

Here are my thoughts on what might be considered for these sections individually and as one combined section.

Leadership: List any relevant organizations you belong to and actively participate in. You don't need to be an officer, but need to be a real contributor. List your results if they are impressive or involved students or schools.

This is also the place to list any awards or honors not appropriate for your education section. Limit them to the most significant and/or recent. You can list more awards on the web, which we will discuss in Chapter Six.

> ### Tracy's Tip!
>
> Many people have a professional development section on their resume with conferences and trainings they've attended. **Delete this section.** It's seen as resume filler for people who don't have enough REAL experience, even if that reality does not apply to you. If it's that important, it can be fit in your education or certification sections. If you presented at a conference, you can list it under leadership.
>
> As mentioned above, we discuss how the web is a better place to list supplemental information like conference attendance in Chapter Six as well as Chapter Four.

Skills: I usually recommend deleting a separate skills section on most teacher resumes unless they are applying for a technology position or to a school with a technology focus. As a college graduate, it is assumed that you know how to use the programs in the Microsoft Office Suite, as well as search the internet, so don't list those as skills.

Affiliations: If you are a member of any professional education associations, you could list them, but this is often the first place to cut when you are short on space.

> ### Tracy's Tip!
>
> **References do not belong on your resume.** References are provided later in the process or through specific fields on the application. It is a good idea to decide whom your references will be, let them know, and create a pretty references document with that information. You also do not need to include the words "References available upon request" on your resume. It takes up space you need for your accomplishments, and it's a given that you'll provide references if and when I ask.

Okay, that's a wrap on creating your extraordinary resume section by section. You should now print out your resume and review it with a critical eye for typos and extraneous words. If you are struggling with page length, the next chapter is all about formatting.

You should also review your resume to make sure you haven't undersold yourself. Let humility take a backseat when it comes to the job search. A 2012 research study out of the University of Nebraska-Lincoln reported that interviewees who scored high on an inventory of narcissistic traits were more successful in being hired than those who were perceived as humble. While truly being a narcissist—someone who is delusional about his or her abilities and has a hard time believing he or she can do anything wrong, for starters— is bad, it is **scientific evidence** that hiding your awesomeness gets you nowhere.

Talk about the amazing stuff you can do for others in your resume and you'll be rewarded.

CHAPTER THREE EXERCISES

Here is a checklist of the tasks discussed in this chapter that will help you create your extraordinary resume.

Task	Done? Check off enthusiastically once the answer is yes!
1. Create your contact information section with special attention to your email address.	
2. Draft a summary statement if you choose to use one.	
3. Delete any objective section.	
4. List your education in the proper order with correct honors and achievements.	
5. Check your certification section to make sure your current and anticipated certificates are listed clearly.	
6. Decide if you will include more than one experience section.	
7. Draft the experiences you will include, focusing on parallel structure, action verbs, and quantified results.	

8. Review specific teaching accomplishments, especially those from student teaching if you are a new graduate or career changer, and add relevant keywords as appropriate.	
9. Review and edit your leadership, skills, and affiliation section(s).	
10. Eliminate any language about references.	
11. Print your resume and relentlessly delete extraneous words and bullet points while checking for typos, consistency in grammar and punctuation, and unneeded humility.	

Chapter Eight includes two sample resumes—one for new teachers and career changers and one for experienced teachers. Let's keep going!

CHAPTER FOUR: MAKING YOUR RESUME PRETTY

Announcement: **this is the most important chapter in the entire book.** If you don't have a resume that is visually appealing, the words on it do not matter.

As I confessed earlier, I sometimes read less than half of the resumes submitted for a competitive teaching position because I am forced to make tough decisions about my time. If I open your resume and it looks cluttered and it is too hard to figure out who you are in 10 seconds or less, I Do Not Read (DNR) it. In this case, DNR also stands for Do Not Resuscitate as that was your only chance to get my attention.

Let me reiterate: you may have awesome experience that is an exact match for the teaching position, but you're not going to be hired if the recruiter does not read the resume you send. You may have been teacher of the year and won two Pulitzers, but if it's buried in the document, no one will know.

How you format your resume is the most important thing you can do to ensure that you hook your dream job.

Experienced recruiters' brains are programmed to quickly toss a resume without reading a word based on the aesthetics. When I open a document, I subconsciously ask myself the following

- Is there a reasonable amount of text on the page?
- Does it look like the formatting will allow me to easily scan for what I need?

If the answer is "no" to either question, the resume goes into the trash bin before I've even read a word.

My fifth teacher recruiter confession: I never feel guilty about tossing confusing and ugly resumes. Submitting a well-formatted resume tells me something about your organization skills, how you make decisions, and how you process information- all critical skills for effective teaching.

An extraordinary resume is easy to read.

When I talk about pretty resumes, I am talking about resumes that are well-designed and polished. They are visually appealing and easy on the eyes.

What aesthetic choices do I have to pay attention to?

Aesthetics is the philosophy of design, art, and beauty. The philosophical and practical choices you make regarding the aesthetics of your resume are crucial. In particular, there are five important design choices to make.

- Alignment
- White space
- Font
- Bullet points
- Headers and titles

Let's review each of these aesthetic choices in detail. Remember that I have included two resume examples in Chapter Eight to help you visualize these suggestions.

Tracy's Tip!

Making the suggested aesthetic changes to your resume may prompt some funky things to happen to the document, such as forcing your resume onto an extra page. Go back to Chapter Three for ideas on how to edit your text and make specific language choices to make it all fit within the visual framework.

Always print your resume to check for typos and formatting errors. You'd be surprised how different things look from format to format, even in PDF.

- **Alignments:** The human eye scans from left to right in an F formation. This means that any text that is heavily indented or centered takes longer for me to scan...and that makes me cranky. It means that you've increased the odds I'll delete the file immediately.

  Align your contact information, sections, and descriptions left. Don't indent or center. The dates and locations in your experience and education experiences should be flush right.

- **White Space:** Never use bottom, left, or right margins smaller than .5" or higher than 1.0". If you have small margins, reviewers will find that the page is too dense to read. Likewise, margins over 1.0" would make me question your work ethic and maturity. If you went to school for four years, you should have participated in enough activities and had at least enough part-time work experience to fill a page.

  One way to determine if you are using white space appropriately is to print your resume and hold it at arm's length. **What do you see? Is it balanced and aligned or does text look jumbled?**

  Finally, make sure there is enough space between section headers and experience titles. It can be a very tight amount of space, but white space is needed to provide visual cues for the scanning experience.

  We discussed this in Chapter Three, but it's perfectly acceptable to put your contact information in the header of your resume to save space. Be sure your contact information is not too close to the top of the page, and double check how this section appears when the resume is printed.

- **Font:** Never use a font size less than 10 point. Your ideal is 11 or 12 point font. I wear bifocals and small fonts make me dizzy. Headers and contact information can be larger.

  Most old-school resume experts would say to only use the Times New Roman font for your resume, but I am a fan of using diverse fonts. When everyone uses Times New Roman, the resumes blend together in my pile. I recommend using a serif font such as Cambria, Georgia, or Garamond. Stick to one font for your entire resume. Don't use anything too informal.

- **Bullet Points:** Use bullets to list all items under a job or under your leadership, skills, and affiliations section(s) (see Chapter Three). Since people first scan resumes, bullets act as visual guides to help with that scan.

- **Headers and Titles:** Headers provide a visual cue to the reader that you are moving from one section of your resume to another. Headers should use a slightly larger sized font. You may also use a navy blue or dark gray color for your headers.

  Titles are where you name your role at the job or university you attended and indicate to the reader that you are now going to describe a new experience. Titles should be the same size as your accomplishment bullets.

Both headers and titles should be bolded. Be wary of heavy underlining.

MORE AESTHETIC RULES

- **Do not use an electronic resume template.** Using a template gives the impression that you don't know how to use a computer. Plus, most Microsoft Word templates do not use the clean formatting rules described in this chapter.

- **Choose the right number of pages.** This was discussed in Chapter Three, but if you have less than ten years of experience, your resume should be one page. I read maybe 10% of second pages on resumes. Even if you are experienced, get all the important information on page one. If you have a master's degree with significant academic experience (a publication, teaching assistantship, etc.), you can also get away with two pages.

- **Less is more. Concise is critical.** Look for bullet points that are wordier than others and for any jobs that have more than four bullets. These are the places to cut back.

- **Realize the web is your friend.** If you have accomplishments on your resume that you don't want to let go, but know you have to in order to meet aesthetic requirements, you can create an online presence to capture those accomplishments. In Chapter Six, we'll discuss the basics of how you can direct people to your LinkedIn profile or digital portfolio for more information.

Creating a pretty resume will convince a recruiter or principal to take time to learn about how extraordinary you are.

CHAPTER FOUR EXERCISES

Here is a checklist of the tasks we discussed that will make your resume pretty.

Task	Done? Check off enthusiastically once the answer is yes!
1. Align all your text left, except dates and locations which are flush right.	
2. Print your resume and hold it at arm's length to judge your use of white space.	
3. Adjust margins to be between .05" and 1.0".	
4. Check that there is enough white space between headers and titles.	
5. Adjust the font size of your contact information and print it to ensure it appears correctly.	
6. Check that everything that should be bulleted is and that they are all aligned.	
7. Choose a slightly larger font size for your headers and bold them.	
8. Bold your titles and ensure that they are the same size as your accomplishment bullets.	

9. Check that your resume is the right amount of pages for your experience level.	
10. Decide what accomplishments and activities belong on the web and move them there.	
11. Print your resume and relentlessly delete extraneous words and bullet points while checking for typos.	

CHAPTER FIVE: THE TRUE PURPOSE OF COVER LETTERS

My sixth confession: I haven't read a cover letter in at least five years. And I know I am not the only recruiter who can say this.

Cover letters don't tell me much. As an experienced recruiter, I can assess your writing skills through your resume and often a more targeted writing sample that I will send to you or require as part of the application process. Anything I want to know about your motivations and why you are a great fit for the job will come in an interview.

Frankly, I was not going to include a lesson about cover letters as part of this book, but I've found that people **freak out** over cover letters. Plus, most application processes still require them. Even though the title of the document makes you think the cover letter is an introduction that provides a cover for your resume, recruiters and hiring managers read the cover letter **after** the resume.

Here is how cover letters are used 90% of the time, if they are used at all.

- Recruiters and hiring managers receive a resume (Chapter One). If it looks easy to read, they'll scan it (Chapter Four).
- They'll scan it to look for patterns, transferrable skills, and quantifiable accomplishments that go with the job and/or organization. If they see those things, they'll read it more slowly (Chapters Two and Three).
- If they like your resume, they'll read your cover letter and do one of the following:
  - Confirm their thoughts that you are a good candidate.
  - Eliminate you because you don't have a good grasp of formal writing.

The bottom-line: the cover letter is a writing test.

> **Cover letters are used to verify a judgment already made about you.**

> **Tracy's Tip!**
>
> If writing is a challenge for you, keep your cover letter short. When I write an introductory letter, I try to make it as short as possible to minimize the possibility of error.

What should I say in my cover letter?

A cover letter should be three paragraphs. You can pre-write these and then change the details for each job that you apply to.

Paragraph One: Your opening should be about the school and not you. It addresses why you want to work there. Here's an example.

I am pleased to submit my application for the open Teacher of Mathematics position at West Beverly Hills High School for the 2013-2014 school year. I am committed to helping students excel in math, and I am inspired by the West Beverly Hills High School's school-wide dedication to helping its students pursue STEM careers. The information I found throughout your website has led me to want to join your team.

Separate from the act of writing a cover letter, you should research schools to find out if you are a good fit for that organization. Other than searching the school's website, you should also search Google for the school and principal's name. You can also set up daily Google Alerts for these terms so that new ones will be emailed to you. Use the **specific findings and school values** that inspire you to write the first paragraph of your cover letter.

Paragraph Two: Your next paragraph is about why you became a teacher, what you can do for the school, and how your expertise makes you a good fit. This paragraph should not regurgitate things that the hiring manager already read on your resume. Another example...

Last year, I switched careers and began the training process to become a teacher. I realized how important my K-12 teachers were to my own success in life and felt compelled to return that gift to today's generation. I know that my intensive, hands-on training through my Awesome School Fellowship coupled with my professional experience as an accountant will help me teach West Beverly Hills High School's students to learn and love the math they need to succeed now and in their future careers.

If there is something very specific from your student teaching experience that would help you with this school's population, you should mention it in this second paragraph. This is also the place to address anything specific and interesting in the job posting. However, keeping it basic will do and help you pass the writing test.

Paragraph Three: Use your closing section to reiterate how interested you are and how to contact you. A final example...

I am eager to meet with you to discuss the position, including how I think I can be a great member of your team and help you achieve your mathematics goals for your students. I can be contacted at (444) 333-5555 or yyyy@xxx.com. I look forward to hearing from you at your earliest convenience.

Cover letters are formal letters and you should follow a business letter format when writing them. They should also be addressed to a principal's name, which is found on the web. If you are applying to a district to be considered for many positions, it would be addressed to the director of human resources or director of recruitment, also found on the web.

Many recruitment experts recommend spending more time customizing your cover letter. I think it's a better use of your time to focus on making your resume extraordinary and specific, as well as other job search activities like networking.

Your extraordinary resume gets you an interview. A basic, clean cover letter eases the way.

CHAPTER FIVE EXERCISES

Here is a checklist of the tasks we discussed to help you create cover letters.

Task	Done? Check off enthusiastically once the answer is yes!
1. Write a sample cover letter using the three paragraph format suggested and save the file in your storage system (Chapter One).	
2. Before submitting any cover letter, print it and relentlessly delete extraneous words while checking for typos. Pay special attention to potential typos in the addresses and salutation.	

A sample cover letter is included in Chapter Eight.

CHAPTER SIX: THE BENEFITS OF SOCIAL MEDIA AND DIGITAL PORTFOLIOS

Most of the education industry is stuck in the old-school recruiting world where recruiting efforts are focused on career fairs and the "post-and-pray" strategy where you place vacancies online and hope that the best candidates find them. Organizations in other industries spend more resources on social recruiting, which includes using social networks such as LinkedIn and Twitter, as well as websites and blogs, to source and communicate with great candidates who might not have applied to a posted job.

There are trends that show schools are moving toward adopting social recruiting strategies. That's a good thing, too. Social recruiting is highly cost-effective, more teachers are engaging in online activities, and research shows that recruiters are likely to find high performers by searching social networks. In 2012, the *Journal of Applied Social Research* published the research finding that employees who were consistent users of social media were more likely to demonstrate behaviors and transferable skills that were positively correlated with academic and job performance compared to those who did not engage in online networks.

Some psychologists have even suggested that those without a Facebook profile are considered suspicious. That may sound extreme, but I agree in principle.

My seventh confession to you: once I start communicating with a candidate directly via email, usually at the interview stage, I check their online activities and make judgments about them based on what I find…or don't find.

Looking for information about teacher applicants online doesn't take much effort on my part. I use a handy Gmail add-on called Rapportive that shows me which LinkedIn, Twitter, and Google+ profiles are connected to the email address associated with any message I receive. Recent activity on those networks appears in my right sidebar. Someone who used Rapportive and received an email from me would see the information in the image below.

Rapportive Sidebar Example

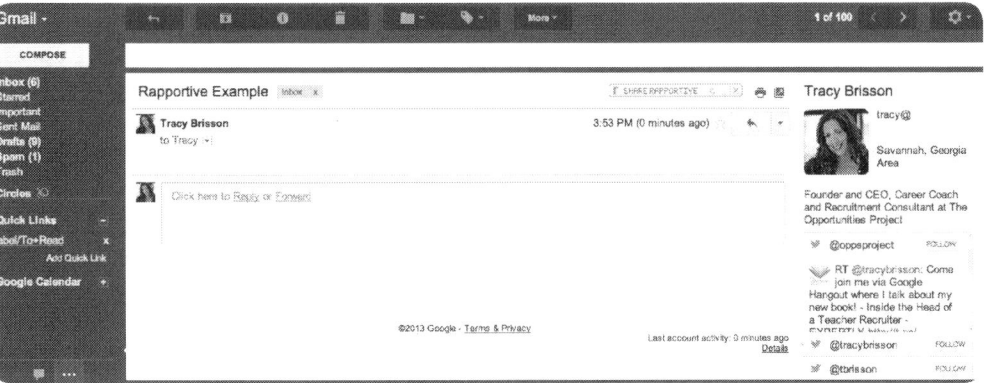

Rapportive has exposed amazing information about teacher candidates to me. Once, I saw a Twitter profile picture pop up that I cannot describe to you without slapping an X rating on the cover of this book. Another teacher emailed me (on his iPhone with lots of those autocorrect abbreviations I mentioned in Chapter One) to indignantly ask why I hadn't contacted him about an interview. When I glanced at my Rapportive sidebar, I saw his last three tweets were expletive-riddled threats to one of the *Real Housewives of New Jersey*. Classy. His message was quickly sent to my trash without a reply.

Crazy stories are fun to share, of course, but I also worry when I receive a message from someone who seems unconnected to any social networks. I instantly become lukewarm about his or her candidacy. Why isn't that person demonstrating intellectual curiosity and using the tools available to them to engage in their professional world online? Remember when we talked about that in Chapter Two?

It's to your advantage as a teacher to be at the forefront of the social networking trend in education.

Do the following when it comes to using social media and online tools to compliment your extraordinary resume.

- Create a digital portfolio or landing page for your professional endeavors.

- Create a LinkedIn profile connected to the email address you'll be using for your job search.

- Consider participating in education conversations on Twitter.

Detailing every step for creating a perfect online portfolio and LinkedIn profile is outside the scope of this guide, but the rest of this chapter provides sufficient information to get you started using these tools.

Why do I need a digital portfolio?

A typical digital portfolio is a multi-page website that shows your potential for teaching and is a great tool to facilitate your job search. It can include a bio, a link to your PDF resume, examples of lesson plans, references, descriptions of student work, details about your professional past that were edited out of your one-page resume, pictures, and other pieces of information that are important for potential employers to know about you as a teacher. Find out the rules from your employer, student teaching site, or university before posting student work or pictures online.

Some universities have students complete digital portfolios as part of their teacher preparation program. Most of those portfolios look like student projects and don't give me the information I need. For example, I actually don't care about your educational philosophy, a standard requirement for many of these university-based portfolios. An independently-constructed digital portfolio that markets your strengths and results is what is important to me as a recruiter.

> **Extraordinary professionals are not afraid to publicize their value.**

The following is a screenshot from a digital portfolio that Ms. A., my client, used to land her teaching job in Queens, New York. In 2010, Ms. A. applied to dozens of jobs online with no response. More than anything, the process made her feel discouraged about her abilities. I suggested that she develop a digital portfolio that highlighted what she knew she did well to boost her confidence. She could also email the link to her portfolio directly to people in her network.

A week after finishing her digital portfolio, Ms. A. met a principal at a party. She realized that she had applied to a job at his school but had never heard back about it. It didn't seem appropriate to ask about it right there, but she was able to get his email address and send him a quick message the next day. She told him how much she enjoyed meeting him, that she was a certified English teacher seeking an opportunity, and that she wanted to share a link to her digital portfolio that demonstrated her teaching strengths in case he had openings.

The principal emailed her back immediately and set up an interview. He told her he loved how she used humor in the lesson plans she featured on her site such as the one titled "So, a noun walks into a bar...." He also said that teachers who used humor did well in his school. She was hired and is still teaching at this school three years later.

Example of a Digital Portfolio

Ms. A.'s story illustrates two of the best reasons to have a digital portfolio: it displays your personality in a way a resume cannot, and it is a non-invasive way to circulate information about yourself to people you may not know that well.

Sending an uninvited resume to someone is pushy. Sending a link to something interesting to read is charming.

Even though her resume was extraordinary (I helped her with it!), I am not sure Ms. A. would have been selected via the posting process simply based on the number of applications the school received. The digital portfolio was critical to her success.

How do I create a digital portfolio?

The digital portfolio in the screenshot above was used creating **Blogger,** a free Google site for blogging and websites. Another free site that I suggest is

Wordpress.com. You can create stand-alone pages, including an about page, in addition to or in substitution of blog posts on both of these platforms. They are easy to use and there are many free guides on how to best use them for portfolios.

Many teachers also use the blogging platform **Tumblr** to create their teaching portfolios and also engage in conversations via "tags" about education and teaching within the site.

For example, this link would provide you a list of all Tumblr posts currently tagged "#student teaching": http://www.tumblr.com/tagged/student%20teaching. Much of it may not be relevant (or appropriate) for you, but take a look to get ideas for your own portfolio, as well as for your resume and interviews.

Barbara Siemens (http://barbarasiemens.tumblr.com/) uses Tumblr for her teaching portfolio as shown below. She says, "Tumblr provides a casual setting for education professionals to exchange research, support, and best practices. Additionally one can establish an online presence in your field, and receiveconstructive feedback on that presence."

Example of a Tumblr Portfolio

Tracy's Tip!

You can publish the PDF version of your resume online using Dropbox or Google Drive and link to it in a digital portfolio or in an email. If you are using Dropbox, go to the website for your account and find your resume file. Click the link icon associated with the file and then the "Get Link" button on the next screen. In Google Drive, open the file and click the "Share" button. Change "Private" to "Anyone with the link."

Dropbox and Google Drive produce long links. If you are sending a link to your resume in an email, you can shorten it using a free service such as Bit.ly before copying and pasting it into the message.

You can also use an off-the-shelf personal landing page to display your critical professional information. Flavors.me is a free service that helps you create a unified web presence, meaning it integrates your social media profiles, other links, and basic information about yourself onto one page. For $20 a year, you can also use a custom domain name (e.g., your name) for your profile. Many professionals who do not have time to manage a website, or already spend considerable time on social media, choose to have a basic landing page instead of a portfolio. You may also consider a similar service for building landing pages called **About.me.**

I spoke to two teachers who use Flavors.me as their landing pages. They have varied approaches, but they all generally highlight their LinkedIn profiles, their Twitter streams, and links to Dropbox or Google Drive versions of their resumes. I like how they show their professional personality as teachers through the content they've selected.

Example of a Flavors.me Portfolio

 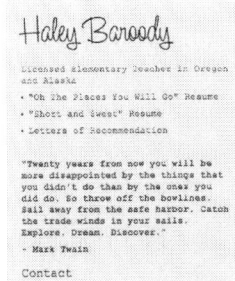

I have highlighted Haley Baroody's profile (http://flavors.me/baroody) above. Haley told me, "I have loved using Flavors.me to promote myself as a teacher. It makes it super easy. Many job opportunities have presented themselves to me, mainly because my website was quick and easy for the person to find everything they needed (resumes and letters of recommendation). As a result, I had an opportunity to teach in Costa Rica and received job offers in Nicaragua and Alaska. I believe I got a foot in the door because of my site."

Teacher John Sowash (http://flavors.me/jrsowash) said, "My personal philosophy regarding web portfolios is to put myself in as many places as possible so that more individuals and organizations can connect with me. Flavors.me has allowed me to leverage the content I have developed (tweets and blog posts) to identify myself as a leader in the realm of educational technology."

Tracy's Tip!

When posting your resume online, take off your address and phone number, and if you must include an email address, write it out as "name [at] domain.com" instead of "name@domain.com." This will prevent spammers from picking up your email address. LinkedIn, Flavors.me, and other digital portfolio platforms all allow people to contact you directly through their sites without publishing your email address.

How do I create an effective LinkedIn profile as a teacher?

In addition to using your extraordinary resume to apply for positions online and connect with people through networking, you should use it to create a great LinkedIn profile.

LinkedIn is a social network focused on networking for professional purposes. It has over 200 million members and thousands of connections are made there every day. You can use LinkedIn to highlight your accomplishments, connect with current and past colleagues, and engage with experts and peers in groups. You can also use its search functionality to research companies and individuals' career paths. Recruiters use LinkedIn to search and contact potential applicants who might not know about their openings.

Why is LinkedIn relevant to teachers? While only a small percentage of teacher recruiters currently use LinkedIn to search for potential hires, you only need one of those people to have the perfect job for you. LinkedIn also has excellent search engine optimization. In other words, when someone searches for your name via a search engine, your LinkedIn profile is one of the first results. This is great for organizations that Google candidates as part of their employee background check process. Finally, you have limited space available on your resume. A LinkedIn profile is a great place to list everything that did not make the cut for your resume.

You can import your current resume to build your LinkedIn profile and make edits in each section. Your goal is to have a strong and complete profile. As you update your profile, LinkedIn's Profile Strength Meter will appear in the right sidebar and give you advice on how to make it as strong as possible.

Complete profiles are 40 times more likely to appear in LinkedIn search results. According to LinkedIn, you need the following to have a complete profile. Almost everything listed is already on your resume.

- Your industry and location
- An up-to-date current position (with a description)
- Two past positions
- Your education
- Your skills (minimum of three)
- A profile photo
- At least 50 connections

I met Detroit-based social studies teacher Amanda Petrarca in the TEACH group on LinkedIn. Amanda has never applied directly for a job she has been hired for, and has always been found online by recruiters representing schools and districts. Amanda's thoughts on LinkedIn: "As an educator who obtain three prior positions through posting my online resume on various sites, I felt it imperative to also have a LinkedIn profile available for industry professionals and administrators to easily access. I believe the networking available through LinkedIn also builds my knowledge, visibility, and connections for future advancement opportunities."

Example of a Teacher LinkedIn Profile

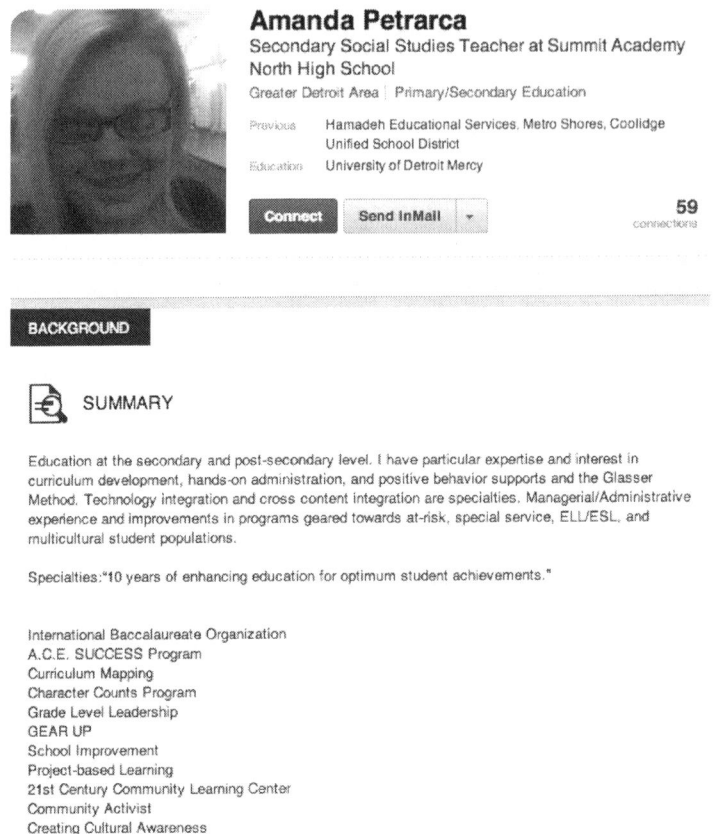

You're saying Twitter is important for teacher networking? Tell me more.

While teachers can be found on all of the social media sites we've discussed, Twitter is one of the more important online networks for teachers. It is simple to create a Twitter profile of 160 characters or less and follow relevant educators that you find through the search tool. In your tweets, you can share links to articles you like, provide your own thoughts about teaching, or reply to people in response to information they shared. If you'd like to stay silent, you can simply read other people's tweets and learn from them just the same.

People converse about common interests on Twitter using hashtags, such as #teacher and #sped (for special education). They also congregate at a specific time to chat about a topic using a hashtag with the word "chat" in it such as #edchat. You can also use the chat tags to call out any tweet at any time of day that you think would be interesting to people who would attend those chats. The screenshot below is list of tweets that appeared when I searched for the #edchat hashtag on a random Tuesday evening.

The #edchat hashtag on Twitter

Why is it important to participate in this Twitter conversation? In Chapter One, we talked about how important it is to have a large network. A large network can include people who you only know online. You could meet a teacher in Boston in a Twitter chat and suddenly find out that she met a principal in your geographical region at a conference and can refer you. Second, you will learn so much from speaking with experienced teachers in this forum and that will only benefit your practice. Your new knowledge will also make you a more interesting candidate in interviews.

If you feel confused and need more direction, no worries. You will be led through a tutorial on following, replying, sharing, and hashtags when you create your Twitter account. Just remember to search for well-known-educators and the #edchat hashtag once you get going.

Tracy's Tip!

Don't be afraid of Facebook, but be smart about how you use it. Facebook is important to me as a teacher recruiter. Since I've worked in education most of my life a significant number of my Facebook friends also work in schools. When I post that I have teacher openings as a status update, I get wonderful candidates recommended to me. In addition, Facebook's primary user base matches the teacher demographic: women who are under 49 with a bachelor's or advanced degree. This makes it a great platform to advertise my clients' teaching positions. So, please, please...use Facebook! Just be sure to follow these rules.

- **Use your privacy settings.** Only accept Friend requests from people you trust. Under the Privacy Settings and Tools, make sure you select "off" for "Do you want other search engines to link to your timeline?" and "friends" for "Who can see my posts?"

- **Remember privacy settings do not protect people's stupidity.** Here's a story for you. My colleague who recruits for a bank interviewed a candidate that a junior employee had recommended. As a courtesy, she visited the employee's cubicle to update him that she was probably going to hire the recommended person. Before she opened her mouth, she saw a Facebook status update scroll across the employee's screen from the interviewee that said "Wow. My interviewer was one hot cougar." Funny or not, his "compliment" continued his unemployment. What you think is private can suddenly be visible in unexpected ways beyond your friends. Be thoughtful about what you post.

- **Tell your Facebook friends that you are looking for a job.** While LinkedIn is supposed to be the social network we use for professional matters, your Facebook friends are people who likely care more about your welfare and happiness. Let them know what is going on with you during this critical time. You will be surprised who will pay attention and who surprisingly knows important people in the education sector.

- **Like the Facebook pages of school districts and charter schools you are considering in your job search.** Many school districts and charter schools manage Facebook pages to provide updates to the community. By liking a page, you'll get more insights into what the school values and what the students are doing. For example, fans of the Facebook Page for the Alma del Mar Charter School in New Bedford, Massachusetts, were treated to photos

> from a recent trip to the theater, a YouTube video of their cheerleaders, and an announcement that one of their teachers had received a fellowship to study in Singapore, all within three days. Anything that you find inspiring on a Facebook page will be great to speak about in an interview or in a cover letter.

CHAPTER SIX EXERCISES

Task	Done? Check off enthusiastically once the answer is yes!
1. Review your current online profiles.	

You likely already use Facebook, Twitter, Tumblr, LinkedIn, Google+, or other social networks. Take a moment to review your profiles to ensure that you feel everything you've posted reflects well on your character and that you are comfortable with your privacy settings. It is also a good idea to Google yourself and see what you find.

Task	Done? Check off enthusiastically once the answer is yes!
2. Research LinkedIn, Twitter, Tumblr, and Google for inspiration for your online properties.	

As I've shown in this chapter, there are many teachers who market themselves online. Schedule an hour to search for portfolios and profiles. Make a list of what you like and don't like about each one you find. How might your findings influence changes to your own online presence?

Task	Done? Check off enthusiastically once the answer is yes!
3. Plan the construction of your digital portfolio.	

Creating a digital portfolio is a multi-stage project. Try to have as much fun as possible with each of these steps.

- Experiment with the different platforms recommended here and decide which one seems most intuitive to you.

- Decide what pages you'll feature on your portfolio (e.g., About, Favorite Lessons, etc.).

- Outline content for each page.

Task	Done? Check off enthusiastically once the answer is yes!
4. Create or update your LinkedIn profile.	

Pay attention to the Profile Strength meter and the components needed for a complete profile.

Task	Done? Check off enthusiastically once the answer is yes!
5. Schedule an hour each week to network professionally on Twitter.	

Check out what educators are talking about and chime in!

A disclaimer: I am recommending the profiles featured in this chapter based on research and conversations conducted in March and April of 2013. I have great faith that these teachers will remain awesome and not post hateful or inappropriate content on their landing pages or social network feeds after I publish this book.

The next chapter discusses what happens next in your job search: putting yourself out there and managing the anxiety that comes with it.

CHAPTER SEVEN: TIPS FOR OVERCOMING JOB SEARCH ANXIETY

So you've created your extraordinary resume, developed your cover letter template, and have a plan for maximizing your online presence. Now you have to take all that and start applying to jobs.

Oh no.

Conducting a job search is an anxiety-inducing activity for almost everyone, no matter how confident you are in your abilities. You must put yourself out there to strangers to judge you against others, exposing your vulnerabilities.

Anxiety can make us sway between extreme feelings that prevent us from taking action. First we go to great lengths to protect ourselves, telling ourselves we aren't worthy and then find excuses to not apply to all the jobs we should to prevent experiencing rejection. Other times we hear something we don't like, maybe criticism, and cultivate anger that distracts us from our goal.

When you think about it, it's hard to not want to run away every time you hit the submit button and relieve your stress by devouring a box of Girl Scout cookies. (Maybe I am just speaking for myself?)

No matter what tricks your brain tries to play on you, the reality is that you will have to apply for many jobs this hiring season before you find your perfect match. Depending on the competitiveness of your geographic region, you could submit your resume up to 100 times. Here are a few tips to help keep yourself sane during this nerve-wracking period of your life.

> ## Focus only on what you control: the excellence of your materials.

How do you detach your emotions from the outcome?

You have done everything in your control up to this point: produced excellent materials, been meticulous in following directions, and contacted people in your network. You must realize that what happens next is out of your control. Let it go.

Controlling your emotions is hard, but certain things can help. Controlling your physical body through exercise and meditation can slow your mind and stop it from obsessing about things. Daily journaling about your emotions can also help (see recommendations for journaling tools in the Chapter One exercises). Once you write something down about your anxiety, it is much easier to let it go.

Some people suggest talking out your anxiety, but that is not always productive if it keeps you focused on your worries or what is lacking in your situation. Avoid only hanging out with your fellow job seekers and moaning about how difficult the job search is going. You do not need to breed that negativity even if it feels good in the moment. When you have an opportunity to be around people, focus on planning positive activities.

It also helps to create a daily routine for your job search activities and never say "no" to an invitation to a potential networking event during this critical time.

Tracy's Tip!

Before you start your job search, decide how many hours you want to spend on it per week. If you already have a job or are in school, you may be only to spend a few hours a week. Remember one hour every weekday is still five hours. Even if you have lots of time, it is important to not make it the focus of your entire life.

Create a recurring appointment for your daily or weekly time on your calendar as soon as you decide and measure how long it takes you to apply to jobs, follow-up, and find and attend networking events. Make any necessary adjustments to your time allotment for future weeks.

How can you practice gratitude?

If you focus on every win, even the small ones like finishing your first round of resume edits, it will be easier to stay positive. I use a tool called Grateful160 (http://grateful160.com) that asks me to email back one thing I am grateful for each day in 160 characters or less (the length of a text message). When I am anxious, I am often surprised how many things I still have to be grateful for and it's hard to choose just one.

How can you peacefully accept rejection and understand what it means?

Most people who apply for a job will get rejected. **Repeat: most people who apply for a job will get rejected.**

It doesn't mean that you will not find the right fit for you as your search progresses, but that is how the numbers work. According to The Harvard Business Review, these are successful job search metrics:

- Five or six interviews for every 100 resumes submitted
- A second interview for about every eight first interviews

It helps to be self-aware during the job search and note what you sense is working and what seems to be getting in your way. If you are not getting called for any interviews after you have submitted 25 or more applications, ask a mentor or peer to critique your resume and cover letter.

Remember that there are many reasons why you will not be hired or asked for an interview, and many of them have nothing to do with how good a teacher you can be. Here are a few of those reasons:

- You might feel like you are perfect for a position, but the experienced recruiter knows a teacher with your skill set would never work with the principal of the school, and, unknown to you, he or she is protecting you from future agony.

- Internal candidates have the inside advantage. Someday you will likely be an internal candidate and be grateful for that perk.

- A position is occasionally redefined after it has been posted, or the position was not clearly posted in the first place. In this case, the job is actually not a fit for your expertise. Sometimes the position is even unexpectedly eliminated for budgetary or other reasons.

As a career coach, I want people to be reflective, but I do NOT advocate following up with hiring managers and recruiters if you do not get a job. Of course, it's appropriate to send a thank you telling them how interested you would be in future opportunities, but that's it.

Understand that endless feedback cycles don't help. Asking for criticism from people you don't know and only met you for a short period of time can do more damage to your confidence than good. Also, in most cases, it was not something you did, but circumstances outside of your control that gave someone else a slight edge. I would again suggest asking mentors and peers to take look at your resume, help you review your memory of the interview, and provide any insight they may have.

Focus on what you can control: improve your resume and submit it for as many as good opportunities as possible.

CHAPTER SEVEN EXERCISES

Here are suggested self-care and organizational routines for your job search.

Task	Done? Check off enthusiastically once the answer is yes!
1. Stick to the same schedule for your job search activities every week.	
2. Schedule time to meditate daily.	
3. Schedule time to exercise three times a week.	
4. Journal daily about your emotions and let them go.	

5. Schedule something fun to do with friends and loved ones at least once a week.	
6. Seek out opportunities to network.	
7. Practice gratitude for every win.	
8. Reflect on what is working well in your job search with peers and mentors.	
9. Follow-up with employers who rejected you to thank them and remind them you are interested in other opportunities.	
10. Remind yourself what is in your control and what is not.	

It's time to move to our final chapter.

CHAPTER EIGHT: FINAL DON'TS AND DO'S AND SAMPLE DOCUMENTS

The following is a final recap of the dont's and do's for creating your extraordinary resume, cover letter, and digital portfolios and social media profiles. Document examples can be found at the end of this chapter.

Let's start with the don'ts before we review the do's.

I commit to NEVER do the following during my job search...

☐	Include clip art or photos on my resume
☐	Spend all the time I allocate to job searching to submitting online applications
☐	Freak out about customizing my resume every time I submit it
☐	Clutter my resume with too much information
☐	Stay home and withdraw from my friends and mentors
☐	Send follow-up communication to recruiters and principals without checking for every potential typo
☐	Copy and paste suggested pieces of information from the career center into my resume without customizing it
☐	Use an inappropriate or outdated email address on my resume
☐	Use an objective on my resume

- ☐ Make recruiters and principals guess about my actual certification
- ☐ Hide all of the interesting things I did before I became a teacher
- ☐ Give all the credit for my student teaching experience to my cooperating teacher
- ☐ Include education keywords that actually have nothing to do with my experience to date
- ☐ Use exotic verbs and adjectives that make recruiters giggle
- ☐ List every award I have won since the eighth grade
- ☐ Say that I know how to use Microsoft Office programs or the internet on my resume
- ☐ Center the text of my resume
- ☐ Use a small font that hurts the eyes
- ☐ Use an electronic resume template
- ☐ Recap my entire resume in my cover letter
- ☐ Miss out on the benefits of social media due to fear
- ☐ Post confidential information about an interview process online
- ☐ Threaten reality television stars on Twitter

- [ ] Search for feedback endlessly if I don't get a position
- [ ] Hang out with my friends and whine about our job searches
- [ ] Tackle my job search at random times without a scheduling plan
- [ ] Give up

However....

I commit to ALWAYS do the following during my job search...

- [ ] Demonstrate excellence at every stage of the recruitment process
- [ ] Reflect every day on my progress
- [ ] Make smart decisions about my time
- [ ] Create a concise one-page resume
- [ ] Use a keyword bank
- [ ] Focus on creating a single extraordinary resume
- [ ] Name my resume file using a proper naming convention

- ☐ Keep multiple versions of my resume files and organize them effectively
- ☐ Read all the instructions when I apply to a job
- ☐ Send my resume as a PDF unless otherwise instructed
- ☐ Tell my network that I am looking for a job, even if they are not in education or don't live in my area
- ☐ Accept invitations to parties and events
- ☐ Be patient and practice compassion for the people who are in charge of hiring
- ☐ Communicate formally with everyone I meet in my job search
- ☐ Submit my applications early in the hiring season
- ☐ Tell interesting stories about how I will inspire students
- ☐ Continue to do "interesting stuff"
- ☐ Focus on how I have demonstrated transferable skills and behaviors in my academic and professional endeavors
- ☐ Describe specific accomplishments I have achieved with students
- ☐ List my education and certification properly on all job search documents

- [ ] Seek feedback from peers and mentors
- [ ] Obtain a professional Gmail address
- [ ] Craft a simple summary statement for my resume
- [ ] Quantify my accomplishments and be specific
- [ ] Write about my accomplishments in a consistent and parallel format
- [ ] Be unapologetic about the awesomeness I've achieved
- [ ] Format my resume so it is clean and pretty
- [ ] Flush all of my resume content to the left and use appropriate margins
- [ ] Edit my resume relentlessly to make it concise and easy to read
- [ ] Keep my cover letters basic
- [ ] Open my cover letter with specifics about why I want to work at that school
- [ ] Manage an online presence through a digital portfolio and/or LinkedIn profile
- [ ] Be smart about what I post online
- [ ] Network with other teachers online via Twitter and/or Tumblr

☐	Take care of myself
☐	Journal about my feelings and observations
☐	Practice gratitude
☐	Ask my loved ones for support and encouragement when I need it
☐	Thank every employer who does not offer me a job
☐	Stay positive and confident

Don't forget to let me know how everything works out by contacting me via the outlets I've provided on the final page of the book. And I hope to share more advice and confessions with you in the future. (You'll love my confession about the woman who interviewed for a teacher job through her puppet.)

You got this. Enjoy your job search!

SAMPLE RESUME FOR A CAREER CHANGER OR NEW TEACHER

JOE SMITH
address: 123 Main Street, Baltimore, MD 98765 **phone:** (444) 333-5555
email: joe@yxyx.com **digital portfolio:** http://joe.yxyx.com

EDUCATION
New York University — New York, NY
The Steinhardt School of Culture, Education and Human Development
Master of Education, Anticipated May 2013, GPA 3.5
Major: Science Education
Honors: Awesome Teaching Fellowship

University of Michigan — Ann Arbor, MI
The Gerald R. Ford School of Public Policy
Bachelor of Arts, May 2011
Major: Public Policy
Honors and Activities: Chancellor's Scholar, Global Intercultural Experience Program in Argentina

CERTIFICATION
Certificate of Eligibility in Biological Science, New Jersey, Anticipated September 2013

TEACHING EXPERIENCE
Student Teacher — 09/12-present
The Justin Timberlake Elementary School — New York, NY
- Taught 35 fourth graders through student-centered lessons and created a safe, organized, and positive classroom environment
- Led 95% of students to achieve a B+ or better on an interdisciplinary unit on female scientists for women's history month
- Coached winner of the school district spelling bee
- Participated in 3 school study teams on the Common Core standards

OTHER EXPERIENCE
Researcher — 07/11-08/12
Corporate Science Research Lab — Newark, NJ
- Contributed research to 6 food science studies that influenced 2011 FDA regulations on poultry
- Organized project budgeting and contractor selection process for $5M federal research project
- Designed and implemented department-wide peer-review procedures

Graduate Assistant — 01/09-05/11
Department of Residential Programs, University of Michigan — Ann Arbor, MI
- Served as a mentor, leader, and a 24/7 multi-purpose resource for 30-45 resident advisors

LEADERSHIP AND SKILLS
- Member of St. Joseph's Church Choir, 2009-present
- Fundraising Chair, Junior League 2011-2012
- Fluent in Spanish

SAMPLE RESUME FOR EXPERIENCED TEACHER

JANE SMITH

address: 789Main Street, Indianapolis, IN 56789 **phone:** (555) 444-3333
email: jane@yxyx.com **digital portfolio:** http://jane.yxyx.com

SUMMARY
Veteran math teacher with 5 years of experience leading students in grades 7-12 to master and love mathematics.

TEACHING EXPERIENCE
Math Teacher 09/11-present
Britney Spears Middle School Indianapolis, IN
- Teach customized math curriculum to 100 seventh and eighth grades across ability groups
- Recognized as a 2012 highly effective educator based on student growth and that 85% of students meeting standards
- Differentiate instruction for individual students using assessment data and integrating interdisciplinary content in collaboration with grade-level teachers
- Lead monthly professional development series for peer teachers on the flipped classroom
- Serve as member of school's comprehensive planning team and assist with fundraising, compliance issues and strategic planning

Math Teacher 09/08-08/11
Justin Bieber High School Indianapolis, IN
- Taught advanced calculus to 60 seniors who achieved 100% college acceptance rate
- Awarded Teacher of the Year by student council in 2009
- Led Matheletes Team of 20 students to regional championships

EDUCATION
Indiana University Bloomington Bloomington, IN
Master of Education, 2008
Major: Mathematics Education

Bachelor of Arts, 2006, magna cum laude
Major: Mathematics

CERTIFICATION
Rules 2002 Initial Practitioner License in Mathematics: Middle School/Junior High and High School Settings

LEADERSHIP AND AWARDS
- Presented at the 2012 Association of Supervision and Curriculum Development (ASCD) conference on "Integrating Video into Mathematics Education for Middle School"
- Blog for education sites including Edutopia, SmartBrief, and others, 2009-present
- Serve as member of district-wide committee on Common Core Standards, 2012- present

COVER LETTER SAMPLE

Joe Smith
123 Main Street
Baltimore, MD 98765

April 1, 2013

Mr. Dylan McKay
Principal
West Beverly Hills High School
456 Beverly Hills Street
Beverly Hills, CA 90210

Dear Mr. McKay:

I am pleased to submit my application for the open Teacher of Mathematics position at West Beverly Hills High School for the 2013-2014 school year. I am committed to helping students excel in math, and I am inspired by the West Beverly Hills High School's school-wide dedication to helping its students pursue STEM careers. The information I found throughout your website has led me to want to join your team.

Last year, I switched careers and began the training process to become a teacher. I realized how important my K-12 teachers were to my own success in life and felt compelled to return that gift to today's generation. I know that my intensive, hands-on training through my Awesome School Fellowship coupled with my professional experience as an accountant will help me teach West Beverly Hills High School's students to learn and love the math they need to succeed now and in their future careers.

I am eager to meet with you to discuss the position, including how I think I can be a great member of your team and help you achieve your mathematics goals for your students. I can be contacted at (444) 333-5555 or yyyy@xxx.com. I look forward to hearing from you at your earliest convenience.

Sincerely,
Joe Smith

Tracy's Tip!

If you are sending a cover letter in an email message, you do not need the addresses or date to begin the message. You can begin with Dear Hiring Manager Name:.

ACKNOWLEDGEMENTS

There are many people to thank for their support in helping me finish and publish *Confessions of a Teacher Recruiter.* Here are just a few.

Thanks to specific people who helped me on the creation of this book: **Sara Lancaster of No. 2 Pen** (http://www.no2pen.com/) who served as copyeditor and has helped on projects since The Opportunities Project launched three years ago; **Jamie Kutner** (http://jamiekutner.tumblr.com) who designed the PDF; and **Edward Antrobus of SEAM Publishing** (SeamPublishing.com) who publishes my books for the Kindle and NOOK and has been a great person to work with on many projects.

An extra special thanks to **The Woodrow Wilson National Fellowship Foundation.** They pre-bought copies of this book and continue to grant me the privilege of working with their dedicated teaching fellows, so that they can make a difference in some of our country's neediest schools.

Much gratitude to The Opportunities Project core team, **Tanisha Christie** and **Sera Bishop**, for their help in supporting the company while I disappeared for long stretches to write.

Thanks to **Justin Mathews**, The Opportunities Project's first official team member in late 2010. Without Justin, The Opportunities Project would not exist today.

Thanks to everyone who has worked with The Opportunities Project on our recruitment consulting work, including the Teach Newark team of **Rachel Eckhardt, Denise Ivanoff, Coy Jones, Chanelle Schneider, Shannon Firth, Steven Francisco,** and **Lisa Welsien.** Your dedication to do great work continues to inspire me and influenced pieces of this book tremendously.

Thanks to all the **coaching clients** who have worked with The Opportunities Project over its first three years. I am glad to have helped you on your journey and am always here for you as you rock your professional possibilities.

Thanks to the fellow entrepreneurs in my life who have helped support me: **Dana Leavy** and **Nicole McGarrell** for your bi-weekly accountability calls, and the FastTrac group, especially **Jaison Greene** and **Danielle Lanyard.** Being able to share our stresses and triumphs has been critical to keeping it moving! Also, thanks to my coaches, **Thekla Richter** and **Les McKeown,** for helping me envision and execute on my projects.

Thanks to **everyone from my New York City Department of Education** days who all continue to believe in me, never forget me, and kept it to themselves if they thought I was crazy to leave my job (and maybe still do). Thanks to **my mom and dad, my friends** in New York City and elsewhere, as well as my new friends in Savannah who are some of the fiercest women I have ever met.

Thanks to my biggest fan, **Eve Hyman,** whose enthusiastic belief in my abilities has sometimes been the only reason I haven't given up. Thanks to **Angus Mungal** for emergency Skype calls and regular Facebook check-ins.

Thanks to all the **students from P.S. 528** who have kept up with me on Facebook. You inspire me every day and your presence in my life keeps me striving to be a better person.

And finally, thanks to **Laura Ross** for her help in changing my life and making hugs from **James** and **Lily** available to me when I need them, and to **Josh Nichols** for supporting me in everything I want to do. I am so lucky to have met you and your love and support means more than I can ever say.

ABOUT THE OPPORTUNITIES PROJECT AND TRACY BRISSON

The Opportunities Project is a talent development, coaching, and recruitment consulting agency that helps individuals rock their professional lives and supports organizations that seek to perform at their best. We empower our coaching clients by helping them make decisions, explore possibilities, and create concrete plans so they can command the professional success they desire as quickly as possible. Since opening our doors in 2010, The Opportunities Project has helped over 1,000 individuals reach career success through speaking engagements, workshops, and one-on-one and group coaching. Through our recruitment consulting, we have also helped organizations hire almost 500 new team members in the education industry.

The Opportunities Project is led by **Tracy Brisson, Founder and CEO.** Before launching her own company, Tracy worked in recruitment for over a decade, including as Director of Teacher Recruitment for the New York City Department of Education, one of the largest employers in the United States, where she supervised the hiring of over 5,000 teachers annually. During her tenure, Tracy's team won second place in the annual Best Employer Brand contest sponsored by ERE, an international recruitment association.

In 2011, Tracy published her first book, Create Your Own Opportunities, available on Amazon and Barnes & Noble. Tracy's career advice also regularly appears in print and national media outlets, including the New York Post and Time Out New York, and on Mashable and CBS MoneyWatch. She has also been a featured speaker at many universities and selective conferences, including theBrazen Recruiting Social Recruiting Conference, the CollegeRecruiter.com FedCollege Conference, #140edu, and TEDxCreativeCoast.

Tracy is an alumna of Syracuse University, New York University, and Teach For America. She splits her time between Brooklyn, New York and Savannah, Georgia.

CONTACT INFORMATION

If you found the advice in *Confessions of a Teacher Recruiter* valuable, we would love your help in telling others about it via social media or by giving us a review on Amazon or Barnes & Noble! You can find more information on the book and sign up for updates at http://confessionsofateacherrecruiter.com.

If you would like to hire Tracy Brisson to speak or conduct a workshop, are considering personalized coaching for yourself or organization, or would like more information on our recruitment consulting services, we invite you to schedule a **free consultation call** at http://opportunitiesproject.com/contact.

You can also interact with our team on Facebook at http://facebook.com/oppsproject or on Twitter at http://twitter.com/oppsproject to learn more about our work.

If you have feedback on this ebook or have questions about Tracy Brisson or The Opportunities Project, please email us at info@oppsproject.com.

Made in the USA
San Bernardino, CA
14 August 2017